The Barnabas Factor

STANDING SECURE IN AN INSECURE WORLD

HAL BOEHM

Unless otherwise indicated, Scripture quotations are taken from the *Holy Bible: New International Version®*. NIV®. (North American Edition)®. Copyright 1973, 1978, 1984 by International Bible Society. Used by permission of Zondervan Publishing House. All rights reserved.

Scripture quotations marked NLT are taken from *The Holy Bible, New Living Translation*. Copyright © 1996, 2004. Used by permission of Tyndale House Publishers, Incorporated, Wheaton, Illinois 60189. All rights reserved.

Scripture quotations marked GNT are taken from *The Good News Bible, Second Edition, Today's English Version*. Copyright © 1992 by American Bible Society. Used by permission. All rights reserved.

Scripture quotations marked MSG are taken from *The Message*. Copyright © by Eugene H. Peterson, 1993, 1994, 1995, 1996. Used by permission of NavPress Publishing Group.

Scripture quotations marked NASB are taken from the *New American Standard Bible®*. Copyright © 1960, 1962, 1963, 1968, 1971, 1972, 1973, 1975, 1977, 1995 by The Lockman Foundation. Used by permission.

Scripture quotations marked KJV are taken from the *King James Version* of the Bible.

The Barnabas Factor:
Standing Secure in an Insecure World
ISBN 978-0-88144-319-6
Copyright © 2008 by Hal Boehm
P.O. Box 701676
Tulsa, Oklahoma 74170

Published by
Thorncrown Publishing
7707 East 111th, Suite 104
Tulsa, Oklahoma 74133

Edited by Betsy Williams of Williams Services, Inc., Tulsa, Oklahoma.

Printed in the United States of America. All rights reserved under International Copyright Law. Contents and/or cover may not be reproduced in whole or in part in any form without the express written consent of the Publisher.

DEDICATION

To the lady with whom the Lord has graciously
allowed me to share my journey—
my sunshine, the joy of my life,
my love, and my wife—
Lisa.

And to my new little sunshine, my daughter, Isabella.

ENDORSEMENTS

"It is so encouraging to have friends like Hal and Lisa Boehm whose passion for Jesus Christ drives them. In this book, *the Barnabas Factor*, Hal reveals foundational truths many believers overlook. In order to effectively reach this generation we all need to learn to stand on the strong foundation God designed. In the cultural battle today, youth are looking for the stability of the truth. In his book, Hal outlines our responsibility as a follower of Christ to stand secure on our faith effectively illuminating God's truth to the youth of today."

Ron Luce
President & Founder of Teen Mania Ministries

"After reading the *Barnabas Factor* I had to honestly evaluate many aspects of my leadership and ministry. Hal has taken a relatively obscure figure in scripture (at least from a verse or page count perspective) and shown me the amazing lesson on the impact of this one life and how Barnabas was central to much of the New Testament church. His personal journey along with these insights will set a course for many to follow and find their true identity."

Tom Newman
President of Impact Productions

"*The Barnabas Factor* identifies one of the great struggles in the Body of Christ. As a pastor, I have witnessed the terrible bondage of insecurity and how insecurity stifles growth and ministry in individual lives. Hal does a great job dealing with the many facets of insecurity and gives Biblical answers that will bring a Holy Spirit driven solution that will produce change in every area of our lives."

Pastor John Brady
The Family Church
McAllen, TX

"In this day of leadership crisis in the Church and society, Hal Boehm's excellent and timely book powerfully presents the main ingredients to a fruitful life and ministry: identity, security, and integrity. The author is himself a "son of encouragement" to thousands in many nations of the world. This volume will edify you and strengthen you."

Jim Hodges
President of Federation of Minister's International

"You will be blessed by the elucidation God has given Hal Boehm which clearly shines through his book the *Barnabas Factor*. The exciting insight and tangible truths found in this book are presented in such a way that will keep you interested and focused. I encourage you to look for and enjoy the message God has for *you* personally as you read this amazing book."

Pastor Chuck A. Lawrence
Christ Temple Church
Huntington, WV

*In the first experience of sanctification
we lose altogether the consciousness of our
own identity, we are absorbed in God;
but that is not the final place, it is merely
the introduction to a totally new life.
We lose our natural identity and
consciously gain the identity that Jesus had.*

OSWALD CHAMBERS

CONTENTS

Introduction		11
Chapter 1	Identity Crisis: The Lesson of the Bamboo Tree	17
Chapter 2	He Did What?	29
Chapter 3	Who Am I?	43
Chapter 4	Get Real: The Role of Integrity	53
Chapter 5	Get Vertical!	67
Chapter 6	Under the Pickle?	85
Chapter 7	Risk Takers	107
Chapter 8	What Does God Say?	123
Chapter 9	Mayday! Mayday!	139
Chapter 10	Lift the Lid!	151
Chapter 11	What Really Happened?	171
Chapter 12	Champions for Christ	191
Chapter 13	Give 'em a Second Chance!	217
Chapter 14	The Cloak of Humility	241
Chapter 15	What's Next?	265

*I have chosen you and I have appointed you
[I have planted you], that you might …
bear fruit and keep on bearing,
and that your fruit may be lasting.*

JOHN 15:16 AMP

Introduction

WHEN I WAS A CHILD, we had a big, solid oak tree in our backyard. I used to lean against it and daydream about all kinds of exciting adventures in regions far, far away. Looking up at the clouds, my imagination ran wild as I pictured various formations. *Hey, that one looks like a dog! Those over there look like a train!* Because this tree did not have low-lying branches, I never could climb it, but in my later elementary school years, my dad tacked a backboard to it. Then my favorite tree became the focus of countless hours of basketball. Many of my childhood playtimes surrounded that tree.

Naturally when I think of a solid, steady tree that provides shade, fruitfulness, and joy, I always think of that giant oak from my childhood. But, one day it became infected by blight and began the slow process of withering. Over time, what once had been the picture of stability and strength became unstable, so much so that my dad became concerned that the tree might eventually topple onto our house! I still remember the sad day when he and my uncle took a chainsaw, an axe, and several wedges and brought down the tree. Even though that tree had been such a source of blessing for so many years, when the insecurities grew to the point that they compromised the integrity of the tree, endangering us and our house, the tree had to be removed.

Have you ever felt like that tree, plagued by insecurities that threaten to harm you and those around you? Let's take a quick test. If you were not selected for the job or promotion that you wanted, would you become jealous of the person who did? Do you find it difficult to truly rejoice when others excel, especially when their success exceeds yours? Do you find it hard to serve or love others without expecting anything in return? If so, you may be plagued with *insecurity blight.*

Like the disease that undermined the mighty oak from my childhood, insecurities can make us unstable and even dangerous to others! This is especially tragic because God has designed us to be steady, strong, stable trees of righteousness who reflect His nature! As believers, our true identity is found in Christ, and there is no insecurity in Him whatsoever. We should be the most secure and stable people on the planet! Sadly, however, this is not the case.

As I have spoken with countless Christians in nearly forty nations throughout twenty years of full-time ministry, I have come to the conclusion that this issue of *insecurity* is one of the biggest problems plaguing believers in the

INTRODUCTION

Church today. It has crossed all denomination, financial, racial, and social lines. From the heads of world renowned ministries to average lay people to moms and dads, teenagers and senior citizens, insecurity does not discriminate. In my opinion this blight has reached epidemic proportions and is greatly hindering the unity and growth of the Church around the world.

It is understandable that children growing up in single-parent households are often *insecure,* even if the existing parent is a believer. But even in Christian homes where both parents are present, many young people are rejecting the faith of their elders. Often fathers are too *insecure* in their position as the priest of the home to impart their faith to their children in an attractive manner. *Insecure* mothers often give in to their children rather standing up to them and administering godly discipline. Faulty leadership like this gives the children nothing to follow or aspire to, and the cycle of *insecurity* continues.

Churches are filled with disillusioned believers who have never found their niche in the Body of Christ. Often the problem can be traced to faulty leadership. *Insecure* ministers are often reluctant when it comes to reaching out to mentor and love the people entrusted to them. Sometimes church leaders blame their congregations for bad attitudes. Certainly this can be a problem, but I encourage leaders to examine whether their own leadership could be contributing to or even causing the problem. Are they actually preventing their people from blossoming?

I have personally witnessed Christian leaders destroy great potential in other ministers because they were threatened by the others' success. The culprit? *Insecurity.* Granted, each individual is responsible not to allow offenses to take root, but leaders should not create an environment where frustrations and disappointments are easily turned into bitterness.

In society at large, *insecurity* permeates nearly every facet of life, manifesting in jealousy, envy, and strife. Sadly, Christians are often as guilty as nonbelievers. Could insecurity *not* be at the root? It doesn't help that we are living in incredibly unstable times. Fear is rife, no doubt contributing to the insecurity issues.

It is for these reasons that I have felt compelled to write the *Barnabas Factor.* What is the *Barnabas Factor?* Simply put, it is *being secure with who you are in Christ.* Those who have tapped into this priceless resource are solid, stable, and secure like that mighty oak from my childhood. They are neither easily threatened nor intimated, and are, consequently, very fruitful in the Kingdom of God. They personify what it means to be a Christian.

How did I come upon this revelation? In my search to understand the insecure believers I was encountering all over the world, I knew the Bible held the answer. The Lord led me to discover a New Testament believer who personi-

INTRODUCTION

fied the antithesis of what I was observing. His name—I am sure you have guessed—was Barnabas. In fact I have come to believe that he was one of the greatest leaders in the entire New Testament. The more I have learned about him, the more I have realized that he found something that set him apart from other believers in the early Church, hence the term my wife Lisa coined (after she listened to me teach on this for years) to describe his "secret"—the *Barnabas Factor*. I believe it is the only true antidote for insecurity. The good news is, this security in Christ is the birthright of every believer!

You may be straining to remember who Barnabas was, or perhaps you have no clue about him whatsoever. As you learn more about him, I believe his life will inspire you and help you overcome any insecurities that have hindered you.

In many ways, this book deals with leadership issues; but lest you think that this means it is not applicable to you, I want to suggest that you *are* a leader, whether you realize it or not. It could be at home, work, school, church, or some other avenue. In addition, you are surrounded by unbelievers who are watching you every day. This fact alone automatically puts you in a position of leadership as Jesus commissioned all of us to lead the world to Him. I honestly believe that the material presented here is relevant to all of our lives.

The Barnabas Factor is also for those who have an insatiable desire to be a man or woman after God's own heart as

King David was. If this is not the driving passion of your heart, I pray that through the reading of this book, you will acquire this fire for God. For without that desire, you will never be able to fulfill His dream for your life—the specific purpose for which He created you.

I believe there is much to be learned from Barnabas that will enable you to exchange your insecurities for absolute security in Christ. As this transformation takes place, it will ultimately allow you to impact this generation in a significant manner with the life-changing message of Jesus Christ!

My greatest passion is to see the earth full of the knowledge of the glory of the Lord as prophesied in the Bible! (Hab. 2:14.) In order for us to accomplish this divinely inspired task in our generation, however, we must deal with and overcome this issue of insecurity that has long kept us divided. As we do, I am confident that we will ultimately become the secure, radiant, triumphant Church of the Lord Jesus Christ, and you will fulfill the unique destiny He has planned for you.

CHAPTER 1

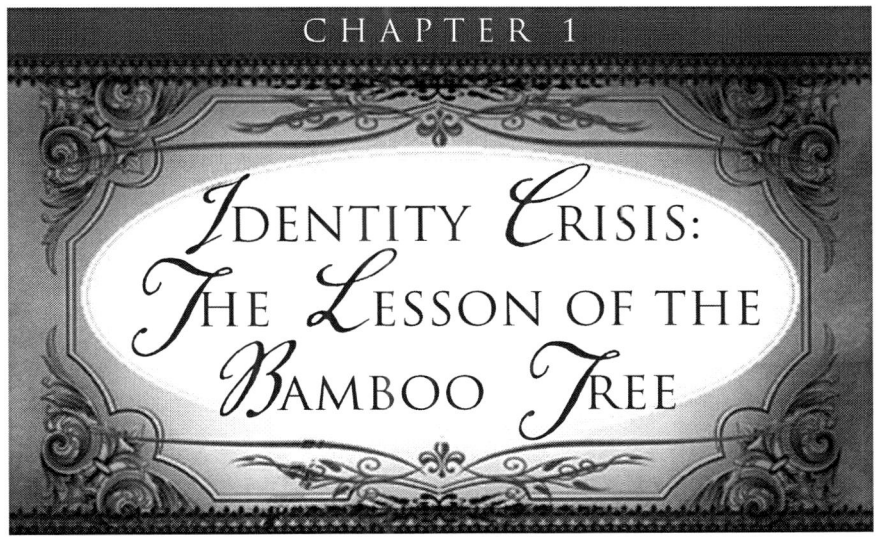

IDENTITY CRISIS: THE LESSON OF THE BAMBOO TREE

WHILE MINISTERING IN THAILAND, I learned a valuable lesson from the bamboo tree. When a Thai farmer plants a bamboo seedling, he will not see any growth whatsoever after a year's time. A full year later, still no change is visible. The farmer will, however, patiently continue to water and tend the seedling for another two years. Then suddenly, in the fifth year, the bamboo plant will begin to grow. In fact, it will develop so rapidly that it can shoot up to two-and-one-half feet each day for six weeks until it reaches some ninety feet in height!

Even though the bamboo tree seems to grow overnight, nothing miraculous takes place. It is not the overnight sensation it appears to be. What then is the secret of the tree's astonishing growth spurt? During the five years when no change is visible to the human eye, the tree is, in fact, developing an extensive root system—many miles long—beneath the surface. The foundation is being established and strengthened to provide for the significant growth that will eventually occur. When the bamboo tree does finally shoot up, its foundation is adequate to sustain its lofty height.

Did you know that you have a great deal in common with a bamboo tree? You may be tempted to grow weary through the years of ups and downs, but all of your experiences—both positive and negative—can be used by God for your benefit. He wants you to have sustained success and be optimally effective. He desires that your character be well established and strong enough to handle the responsibility He entrusts to you.

I believe the growth pattern of the bamboo tree illustrates the importance of taking the time to lay a good foundation in your life. This stage of your development must not be circumvented for any reason or serious problems may manifest in the future and possibly cause much damage to you and others. Jesus spoke to this very issue in Matthew 7:

> "Everyone who hears these words of mine and puts them into practice is like a wise man who built his house on the rock. The rain came down, the streams rose, and the winds

Identity Crisis: The Lesson of the Bamboo Tree

blew and beat against that house; yet it did not fall, because it had its foundation on the rock. But everyone who hears these words of mine and does not put them into practice is like a foolish man who built his house on sand. The rain came down, the streams rose, and the winds blew and beat against that house, and it fell with a great crash."

vv. 24–27

When the storms of life came against the house built on the solid foundation, what happened? The structure weathered each one. The house built on sand, however, came crashing down because the foolish man had not taken the time to establish a firm foundation. This is a perfect example that some shortcuts ultimately cost more than they are worth. Unfortunately there are no shortcuts to maturity.

Chronic Problem

Everywhere I travel throughout the world, I see a chronic problem in the lives of individual believers—including leaders—that has caused much damage. It is an *identity crisis*, and it affects the personal security of its victims. Consider the following:

Why do so many Christian adults become anxious about growing older? Turning forty is a real challenge for many! Could the reason be that the identity of these people has been in their physical appearance, so each wrinkle or gray hair threatens their self-worth?

Why do so many Christian men go through a "midlife crisis"? Could it be that these individuals find themselves at the midpoint of their lives, yet haven't achieved the level of career success they had anticipated? Is their identity based more on what they do than who they are?

Why do so many retirees have a hard time adjusting to that new chapter in their lives, some even passing away soon after reaching the milestone? Could it be that their identity for so long was rooted in their vocations and when that is no longer part of their lives, they are lost with no vision for the future?

Why do so many couples divorce or go through marital problems after their children leave the nest? Could it be that the identity of these couples has been so wrapped up in their children that when the kids are no longer part of their everyday lives, their self-worth and security go away as well?

Why are many pastors and missionaries so possessive of their pulpits or their "turf"? Why do so many not want to become involved in events that are not their idea or don't have their names on them? Could it be that the identity of these individuals is based upon their ministries and if that is challenged in any way, they feel threatened?

Why do leaders who have been given gifted men and women to serve under them seek to control or hide these individuals under a bushel and not allow them to shine? Often these servants leave at the first opportunity, yet the leaders scratch their heads and wonder why.

Identity Crisis: The Lesson of the Bamboo Tree

I have often found myself asking questions like these when I see insecurity so prevalent in the Body of Christ. It is particularly disturbing when I observe it in Church leaders who are easily threatened by the successes of others.

The Revelation

There have been times in my own life when I have felt insecure, yet for years I could not figure out why. During those times, I did not like how I felt around other people and how I viewed myself. Feelings of jealousy, frustration, and anger constantly rolled around inside me and I was easily intimidated.

As I thought about all that the Lord had given me, it made no sense for me to feel like I did. Finally, after dealing with this for some time, I sought the Lord—something I should have done much sooner.

God, in His faithfulness, answered me, revealing that I had built my house on sand and not on the Rock! He then showed me that my *identity* was at the root of my insecurities. It had been misplaced. I had heard it said that people have four basic needs in life: acceptance, identity, security, and destiny. I began to realize that one's *identity* affects his or her personal *security*. That, in turn, ultimately affects *destiny*. For me, this was a major revelation. Very few discoveries have impacted me more.

The Foundation

During this process, the Lord took me back to my childhood and began to show me where my *identity* had been placed on a faulty foundation. As we have discussed in relation to the bamboo tree, the foundation of any structure is important because it provides strength and stability. Consider another example—the construction of a wall. Builders tell me that the measurements of a wall's foundation must be exact. Any deviation from the precise measurements, though not detectable to the human eye, will cause a wall to lean too far one way or the other after it is one or two stories high, making the wall unstable. To ensure that a wall is straight, the builder drops a plumb line to check it. If the angle is off, the wall must be torn down and the measurements of the foundation corrected.

The Lord revealed to me that His plumb line indicated that my foundation was off ever so slightly. After years of building on this faulty base, my "wall" was leaning and beginning to show serious signs of instability. I knew that if I did not correct the identity issue, more serious character flaws would begin to manifest!

In the Beginning

Growing up, I had a good home life with two parents who loved and affirmed me. My father and I had a very special rela-

Identity Crisis: The Lesson of the Bamboo Tree

tionship. We spent countless hours together, during which he mentored and trained me in numerous areas. He believed that quality in raising children meant not only quality time together but lots of it. For these and many other reasons, my father has always had my highest respect, so much so that he was even the best man when my wife, Lisa, and I married.

I mention this because I believe that children receive much of their identity and self-worth from their fathers. Dads have a tremendous responsibility on their shoulders. It is no wonder the devil attacks the family so strongly, oftentimes targeting the fathers.

Why, then, since my own home life had been so positive, was my identity askew? As I continued to seek God about this, He put His finger on the specific area affecting me—athletics. As a young man, I had been an athlete and received a great deal of affirmation as a result. I was proud of my physical abilities. Until this season of soul searching, however, I had not been aware that I had derived most of my security, self-worth, and identity from that role. Participating in sports imparted many wonderful disciplines into my life that I might not have learned any other way, but athletics is not a suitable foundation for a person's identity.

Eye Disease

The fact that my identity was based on this faulty foundation could have gone undetected for much longer, but something happened that forced me to look at this issue head-on. When I was eighteen years old, I developed a rare eye disease known as Retinitis Pigmantosis.

This malady causes the retina to deteriorate from the outside to the center. A person with this condition loses peripheral vision (causing tunnel vision) and most night vision. As the condition progresses, the afflicted may eventually lose sight altogether. To add insult to injury, one in four people with this disease also develops hearing loss; and, yes, I am one of those. My hearing loss is not so severe that I need a hearing aid, but it makes it difficult for me to hear all sounds, especially the ending of words.

Needless to say, all of these symptoms greatly affected my life. For a long time after losing my peripheral vision, I bumped into people and objects constantly, which was extremely frustrating and embarrassing, not to mention painful. I could no longer play sports, and as a result, I ceased to be known as a good athlete.

Of course these difficulties followed me into adulthood and—as I perceived it—even attacked my masculinity. Because I had contracted the disease four years before Lisa and I married, we were aware that potentially, it might grow worse over time. Neither of us, however, fully grasped the significant changes that lay in store. When the disease progressed to the point that I could no longer drive, I had to deal with enormous guilt that my precious wife was married to a man possessing such rapidly deteriorating handicaps.

Identity Crisis: The Lesson of the Bamboo Tree

Lisa, being the wonderful lady that she is, has always been very supportive and encouraging; nevertheless, I hated subjecting her to these challenges.

Learning to depend on others for transportation and having to ask for help with everyday tasks was humiliating—especially at first. This man—who had for so many years received his identity from being a self-sufficient athlete—did not like having to rely on anyone. It felt as if I were in a free fall as I came to terms with my new reality. I did not realize it at the time, but the disease had literally ripped my foundation right out from under me! The disease and all of its effects totally rocked my world.

Who Am I?

In the midst of all of these losses and adjustments, it is no wonder that I struggled with my identity. The constant cry of my heart became, *Who am I?* At the time, I honestly didn't know. Although the answer to this question didn't come all at once, bit by bit the pieces began to fall into place. I am so thankful for my stable childhood and loving, patient wife; for they are the reasons that I was able to adapt as well as I did. All this, however, was not enough to bring me through all the tests I was facing. But God, in His wisdom, knew exactly what I needed. Because of His love for me, He began to gently reprove me and show me where I needed to repair my foundation, so I could begin to put my identity in the right place.

From What, Then?

From what, then, should we derive our identity? The answer is quite simple—from Jesus, the Rock! Most Christians would give you the correct response if you were to ask them, but misplaced identity is subtle. I have observed that many believers *think* their lives are founded on Jesus, but in reality, they base their identity on a myriad of other things. I know this was the case with me.

As has been stated, the foundation of a building and the root system of a tree are the most important parts of the structure. A Bible school director once told of a student who asked him if there was a shorter course he could take to become a minister, rather than the prescribed four-year program.

The director replied, "Well, son, it depends. Do you want to become an oak tree or a squash plant?" After a moment of hesitation, he continued, "When God wants to create an oak tree, He takes many years, but when He wants to grow a squash, He only takes six weeks."

What about you? Do you want to be an oak tree—solid, steady, and fruitful for decades—or a squash plant—here one day and gone the next? The choice is yours!

Identity Crisis: The Lesson of the Bamboo Tree

It Is a Process

Writing a book on this subject has an inherent danger associated with it of which I am well aware. Others may accuse me of arrogantly thinking that I have arrived and that I am always the secure man that I should be. While I wish that were true, growth is a process. Today, I still struggle with the eye disease; and although the Lord has brought me a long way in the area of insecurity, occasionally something will come up that I must deal with. The difference is, now I know to recognize insecurities and am better equipped to resolve them.

If you think about it, the Christian life as a whole is a growth process, and despite the fact that we never quite reach perfection in this life, we continue to strive for it. The first step is to take the time to lay a proper foundation upon which the Lord can build. I write this in all humility, realizing my own frailties and limitations, but always cognizant that God's grace is more than sufficient for all my needs!

It is through the life of Barnabas that the Lord has taught me many of the lessons concerning *identity* and *security* that I want to share with you. Next we will examine an event in the life of Barnabas that reveals how secure he was and how a solid foundation really does affect all that we do.

Lord, I realize that the only way I will ever fulfill my destiny or become the person You have designed me to be is to find my identity in You alone. Help me to recognize areas where I have built on sand, then show me how to correct my foundation so that my life is built on You, the only truly solid foundation. Open the eyes of my understanding so that I see myself from Your perspective, then help me to identify with and stay true to that image. Amen.

CHAPTER 2

He Did What?

AS WE WILL SEE, our correct identity in Christ can lead us to do incredible exploits for the Kingdom of God! Knowing who we are in Christ has far-reaching implications, affecting everything we do and how we view the world around us. In this chapter we will examine several passages from Acts that aptly illustrate this point.

> In the church at Antioch there were prophets and teachers: *Barnabas,* Simeon called Niger, Lucius of Cyrene, Manaen (who had been brought up with Herod the tetrarch) and *Saul.* While they were worshiping the Lord and fasting, the Holy Spirit said, "Set apart for me *Barnabas and Saul* for the work to which I have called them." So after they had

fasted and prayed, they placed their hands on them and sent them off.

Acts 13:1–3 (emphasis added)

This prayer meeting took place in the city of Antioch, located in modern-day Syria. Even though many believers were already involved in taking the Gospel to the nations, most today look to this event as the beginning of the Church's worldwide thrust to the nations. In fact, this is where the apostle Paul (here called *Saul*, his Hebrew name) began his first missionary journey, changing the face of the Church—and ultimately the entire world—forever!

Notice the order of the names stated in the passage. Of the prophets and teachers listed, Barnabas is mentioned first and Saul is mentioned last. In verse 2, even the Holy Spirit mentions Barnabas first! Why? In the eyes of the churches at Jerusalem and Antioch, Barnabas was the leader of the duo. We commonly think of Paul as being one of the most important leaders of the New Testament. While that is true, if we back up a couple of chapters, we read that toward the beginning of the revival at Antioch, Paul, in fact, assisted *Barnabas* in teaching the new believers there:

> News of this [revival] reached the ears of the church at Jerusalem, and they sent *Barnabas* to Antioch. When he arrived and saw the evidence of the grace of God, he was glad and encouraged them all to remain true to the Lord with all their hearts. …

He Did What?

> *Then Barnabas went to Tarsus to look for Saul, and when he found him, he brought him to Antioch.* So for a whole year *Barnabas and Saul* met with the church and taught great numbers of people.
>
> Acts 11:22–23, 25–26 (emphasis added)

After reading this, I think it is likely that at this time, Barnabas and Paul shared a mentor/protégé relationship—Barnabas the mentor, and Paul the protégé. At the very least, Barnabas was Paul's sponsor, his approval giving Paul widespread acceptance among the believers in Antioch. Prior to this, they were not familiar with Paul. Likely, Paul's relationship to Barnabas here laid the groundwork for the relationship Paul would later have with Timothy, his spiritual son. (See 1 Tim. 1:2.)

It is interesting to note that after Barnabas and Paul had been sent forth from the church at Antioch, these two men traveled directly to Cyprus, Barnabas' home. (Acts 4:36; 13:4.) I can only speculate that this is an indication that Barnabas was still the leader at that time, although things were about to change.

A New Thing

While the two men were in Cyprus, God did some amazing miracles through Paul. (vv.6–12.) I believe it was during this time that God showed Barnabas and Paul a new leadership structure for their apostolic missionary band. A

change in the structure was needed because the context of their ministry had changed—from local church to missions.

Notice what the Scripture reveals next:

> From Paphos [in Cyprus], Paul and his companions sailed to Perga in Pamphylia, where John [Mark] left them to return to Jerusalem.
>
> v. 13:13

Did you catch that? A shift takes place here, so subtle that the casual reader might miss it, but I believe it is one of the most profound statements in this book. Note that the verse says, "Paul and his companions." Wait a minute! What happened to Barnabas? Up until this point in the storyline of Acts, the two had been listed as "Barnabas and Saul."

People often miss this aspect of the verse because they usually focus on John's (Mark's) departure, speculating on why he left. Mark's leaving is significant because it later impacts the relationship between Barnabas and Paul, but we will explore that facet of the verse in another chapter. The point here is that the focus of the narrative changes from the ministry of Barnabas to that of Paul. Whereas the pair had been described as "Barnabas and Saul," from this point on, they are mostly referred to as "Paul and Barnabas," Paul's ministry becoming the focus for the remainder of the book of Acts.

He Did What?

Understand the Context

One possible reason for the switch is that the author of Acts, Luke, may not have even known Barnabas personally.

"Then, why did he talk about Barnabas so much up to this point?" you ask.

Understanding some background on the book of Acts will help to explain. It is a widely held belief that Acts was written by Luke; however, many commentators have postulated that up until this point—Acts 13—he received his material from the accounts of others, as he did when he wrote the gospel of Luke. The revival at Antioch was a monumental event and because Barnabas was such a key figure in it, it stands to reason that Luke would have heard a great deal about him and written accordingly.

One reason it is believed that Luke may not have known Barnabas personally is that nowhere in Scripture do the two men appear together. There is no evidence that they ever ministered or traveled together.

On the other hand, we know from Acts 16:10 that Luke became a traveling companion of Paul. It says, "After Paul had seen the vision, *we* got ready at once to leave for Macedonia" (emphasis added). Up until this verse in Acts, Luke wrote in third person—using the pronouns he, she, and they; but in Acts 16:10–18 he switched to first person, using the pronouns I, we, and us. Further evidence is also found in

Acts 20:6–16 and Acts 21, as well as in other places throughout the remainder of Acts. I am sure you know from personal experience that there is nothing like traveling with a person to really get to know him or her, so obviously Luke and Paul knew each other well. It would make sense, then, that Luke would major on Paul's ministry.

This brings up another interesting point. You may have noticed that until Acts 13:9, the apostle's name is stated as "Saul," his Hebrew name. However, at this point where it is believed that Luke began writing from firsthand experience, the apostle's name suddenly changes to "Paul," his Roman name. Specifically the verse where this transition takes place says, "Saul, who was also called Paul. …" From this point on in Acts, the apostle is referred to as "Paul."

Apparently those whom Luke interviewed for the first part of Acts were Hebrews, who would naturally refer to the apostle by His Hebrew name, "Saul." Scholars believe that Luke, on the other hand, was probably a Gentile, explaining why in all the firsthand accounts, he referred to the apostle by his Roman name, "Paul."

A Shift in Roles

There is another reason that I believe the emphasis changes to Paul, and I believe it has to do with the time that Barnabas and Paul spent together on Cyprus (v. 4). It appears

He Did What?

that a major shift took place in their roles. As long as the two were centered in the local church setting, Barnabas had a senior leadership position; but when the two were released as an apostolic band to the nations, Paul assumed the senior leadership position and Barnabas willingly took a step backwards!

That is astonishing! Rarely in my experience have I witnessed such a courageous action. For one leader to step back and allow another to take the lead does not usually occur unless retirement is involved.

I believe that Barnabas was a man so secure that he did not need to have his ego stroked as the senior leader of the band. When he realized that the Kingdom of God would expand further with Paul as the leader, he willingly took a step backwards. Although in most people's thinking this probably was not the best career move, I believe Barnabas did it because he had truly placed Jesus first in his heart. Instead of his identity being based on his *ministry*, it was firmly established on Jesus.

Barnabas was not so interested in building his own empire as he was in building the Kingdom of God! Rather than trying to establish a name for himself, he sought to establish the name of Jesus Christ in the nations.

Not Threatened

What a blessing it would be to have more leaders like Barnabas in the Body of Christ today! Men and women who are secure enough in themselves and in their relationship with Christ that they are not threatened by the Pauls who come into their lives. Rather, they willingly mentor—or at least sponsor—these emerging leaders and release them into their callings.

With Barnabas and Paul, when the setting changed, their roles changed to match their callings. In fact, at the beginning of Acts 13, Luke tells us that prophets and teachers were present at the prayer meeting. There is no mention of any apostles. Up until this point, Paul was probably not recognized as an apostle; but when he and Barnabas traveled to Cyprus and began their missionary ministry, Paul's apostolic anointing became apparent. Barnabas recognized it and willingly submitted to it.

Know When to Let Go

Sadly this is an area where the business world is ahead of the Church. In business there are men and women who are *visionaries* or *starters*. These individuals are talented at jump-starting a venture, but they are not as effective when it comes to the day-to-day operations. That is why entrepreneurs commonly sell their companies after only a few years. If they do decide to stay at the helm for any length of time, they understand that to be successful, they must willingly admit their limitations and surround themselves with people who are good at the nuts and bolts of operating a company. They must believe in their people and respect what they have to say. It is one thing to have detail people around you, but it is quite another to actually listen to their input and implement it.

Unfortunately I have seen the opposite take place on the mission field. It is a fact that missionaries often have to work many years to establish a work in an unreached area. Their dedication is necessary and commendable; however, when it comes time to turn the work over to local believers and move on to new lands, they are often reluctant.

One reason is that seasoned missionaries know firsthand how difficult it is to start a new work. Any glamorous ideas they may have had at the outset of their ministry have been replaced by a more realistic view based upon their own experience. There are no rose-colored glasses, and the very thought of starting over may be overwhelming.

It is also possible that the identity issue may have slowly crept into the thinking of the missionary. Without realizing it, they may have been deriving their identity from that work and not know how to function outside of it. And since misplaced identity cloud's one's judgment, these missionaries may even convince themselves that the work would not continue without them, when in fact the locals could probably take it to the next level. Just look at what has happened with the Chinese Church. Since the missionaries were expelled from China in the 1950s, the body of Christ there has literally exploded from a mere one million people to literally *one hundred million!*

Barnabas had to have been a very secure man, his identity found in Christ alone. What else could explain why he so willingly allowed Paul to take the leadership position? Because of Barnabas' ability to let go, Paul was empowered to fulfill His call and turn the world right-side up! Now you can see why the *Barnabas Factor* is so important and powerful! Unfortunately this selfless attitude is missing in most Christian leadership today. Many men and women are gifted and qualified to do great things for the Kingdom of God, but if the *Barnabas Factor* is not part of their character and if their identity is misplaced, an insidious cancer will begin to eat away at their foundation. Eventually it will choke the life out of their ministry if a change isn't made.

Don't Get Hung Up on Titles

Another attribute of people operating in the *Barnabas Factor* is that they do not get hung up on titles. If you remember, Acts 11 explains that when the church at Jerusalem heard of the revival at Antioch, they sent Barnabas to minister to the new believers there. Although Barnabas was obviously an able minister, highly thought of by his peers, the Scriptures only refer to him as an "apostle" one time and that in the context with Paul. (See Acts 14:14.) Paul, on the other hand, refers to himself as an apostle many times in his letters. Even though it is apparent that the early Church viewed Barnabas as an apostle, he did not feel the need to make an issue of it.

Secure people do not feel compelled to remind others of their titles, they just do what they are called to do and leave the conferring of titles to others. Proverbs 18:16 says, "A man's gift makes room for him" (NASB). Even Jesus did not go around proclaiming that He was God, although He certainly was. No, His works proclaimed it for Him. (See His response to the disciples of John the Baptist in Matt. 11:2–5.) Barnabas knew his place and willingly submitted to it. He did not try to be more than he was called by God to be. His own notoriety and fame were not an issue to him. To publish abroad the wonderful name of Jesus was his first priority.

Please understand that it is not my objective to shine a negative light on the apostle Paul for frequently stating his title. It is likely that he was instructed of the Lord to do so to indicate his God-given authority to write the epistles, which were to be included in the sacred canon of Scripture. Or, perhaps it was because Paul was a work in progress, just like the rest of us. Whatever the reason, I think it is important to note that in one of his letters Paul wrote that he was the least of all the apostles. (See 1 Cor. 15:9 KJV.) Still later in his life he penned that he was the chief of all sinners. (See 1 Tim. 1:15 KJV.) Even if titles were important to him early in his ministry, it obviously became a non-issue to him later in life.

The point here is that it is fine and right for others to attach titles to your name, but you should not focus on them yourself. Your focus should be to fulfill God's call on your life.

What about You?

Do you see how important it is to have your identity based on the right thing? Do you see the impact that a misplaced identity could have on your life and how it could affect the lives of those around you? How do you see yourself? What is the first thing that comes to mind when you are asked to describe yourself? This could give you a clue as to the basis of your identity.

You might say, "I'm a mother." Others might describe themselves as a father, a man, a woman, black, white, Hispanic, an American, Asian, a Native American, a carpenter, a lawyer, an engineer, a missionary, or so forth. Others may think of themselves in terms of their personal attributes: intelligent, educated, beautiful, athletic, great personality, or a combination of several of the above.

Allow me to ask another question: What if the label you use to describe yourself were removed from your life? Who would you be then?

Imagine that you have been an engineer by trade but your job has been phased out. Because of your age, you

He Did What?

haven't been able to find another job. All of your adult life you have been known as an engineer. But now, that foundation for your identity has been removed. If this were the case, how would you function? Would this throw your life into a major crisis?

What if all your life you have received affirmation because of your outward appearance, but now, because of a physical ailment or accident, those good looks are now a thing of the past? Would it cripple you?

When a person's identity has been based upon something that has changed or no longer exists, depression usually comes knocking. If this is the case with you and you are tempted to open the door, don't do it! Remember, the labels and titles we use to describe ourselves are only temporary. They are of this world, which will someday pass away. We should not, therefore, derive our identity from them. Our identity should be based solely upon Christ, who alone is eternal. It is in Him that we "live and move and have our being" (Acts 17:28).

The next time someone asks you to tell about yourself, the first thing that should come to your mind is the fact that you are a follower of Jesus Christ. You are a Christian. Your identity must be in Him and Him alone. Any other titles you bear or roles you play are to be secondary, flowing out of that immovable foundation of Jesus.

Don't you think it is time to really know who you are in Christ? Imagine the positive changes that could take place!

For believers, our identity in Christ will be true for eternity, so why not go ahead and move your identity from yourself to Christ now? You will never regret it! I guarantee it!

> *Lord, continue to show me how I can derive my identity from You alone. Help me to see myself as a Christian first and not to define myself by roles I fill or titles that have been assigned to me. Help me to stay sensitive to Your Spirit and not to be threatened by other people or by what You are doing through them. If at any time I am to step aside or step back so that others may lead, give me the grace to be willing and obedient, for only in Your perfect will I find true fulfillment. Amen.*

CHAPTER 3

Who Am I?

AS WE'VE SAID, how you see yourself will ultimately affect everything you do! If you see yourself with Christ at the center of your identity, then the *Barnabas Factor* is indeed operative in your life. Consequently, you will live a life of fruitfulness in the Kingdom of God and possess a strong sense of personal security as did Barnabas.

You might say, "Okay, I'm ready to deal with this. So, who am I? If I take away all of the labels I have used to define my identity, who is the real me? How can I base my identity on Christ?"

I asked the same questions, and the Lord led me to several verses in my quest for answers:

> I have been crucified with Christ and I no longer live, but Christ lives in me. The life I live in the body, I live by faith in the Son of God, who loved me and gave himself for me.
>
> Galatians 2:20

> Those who become Christians become new persons. They are not the same anymore, for the old life is gone. A new life has begun!
>
> 2 Corinthians 5:17 NLT

> You died, and your life is now hidden with Christ in God.
>
> Colossians 3:3

These verses verify that our identity should be in Christ and nothing else. In actuality, however, most Christians have an "I" problem—"*I* am important. *I* deserve to be comfortable. *I* deserve to have my needs met. After all, *I* have rights!" This is especially true for those of us from Western nations.

According to these verses, "I" no longer lives. It is "Christ" who lives. This means "I" died, and all of "I's" selfish ambitions died along with it.

When I went into the watery grave at baptism, all of my selfish ambitions were washed downstream. When I was resurrected, I became a *new person* in Christ Jesus! The old me died, and the new me—this new person in Christ—lives! My life is now *hidden* and all you should see is Jesus! *I* must empty myself of all fleshly thinking and ways. I like how the apostle Paul put it:

Who Am I?

> Your attitude should be the same as that of Christ Jesus:
> Who, being in very nature God,
> did not consider equality with God something to be grasped,
> but made himself nothing,
> taking the very nature of a servant,
> being made in human likeness.
>
> Philippians 2:5–7

It still baffles me that the Creator of the universe would do this! It is awesome to think that the One who gave each of us breath would come to earth as a servant and not in His role as the King of kings. If He could do this, then surely I can follow His example and do the same! I should be so secure that I am comfortable being Servant Hal, rather than striving to be King Hal. Which is greater in the Kingdom of God anyway, a servant or a king? A servant!

You may have heard of a movie that was popular several years ago entitled, *Dead Man Walking*, which told the story of a man on death row. I may not be a prisoner in the penal system, but I literally am a dead man walking! When I gave my life to Jesus, *I* died. Now *Christ* lives—and walks—in me.

Adults grappling with their identity have been known to say, "I'm just trying to *find* myself." Jesus is the only One who can really help a person *find* him- or herself. He revealed the key when He said, "Whoever loses his life for me will find it" (Matt. 16:25). I can testify to the fact that this is true. The more I have yielded to Christ and allowed Him to live through me, the more fulfilled I am. It has been through this process that I have discovered my true identity and destiny.

Temporal Labels versus Eternal Identity

If someone were to describe me to a person who has never met me, he or she might use some of the following words:

- male
- American
- Caucasian
- married to a woman named Lisa
- minister
- missionary

Even though each of these labels is accurate, my identity as a believer is no longer in those things. Now it is simply in Christ. My identity, my security, and even my self-worth are not tied to the fact that I am a married, white, male, American minister. Rather, my identity, my security, and my self-worth are in Christ.

Think about these statements that I can use to describe myself:

- I am a Christian who was born in America.
- I am a follower of Jesus Christ who happens to be the son of Caucasian parents.

Who Am I?

- I am a believer whom God has called to be a minister of the Gospel.

All of the labels one could use to describe me are secondary to who and what I am in Christ. The temporal labels are no longer of primary importance to me. My identity is in Christ.

Not only is my identity no longer tied to the positive or neutral labels used to describe me, it is not tied to any negative labels either. Others may describe you as lazy, unintelligent, clumsy, shy, handicapped, or whatever. But your identity should not be based upon what others say or the opinions they have of you. In fact, it should not even be based on the opinion you have of yourself! Your identity must be in Christ alone and what *God* says about you. *He* says that you are the head and not the tail! *He* says that you are blessed and highly favored! *He* says that you are more than a conqueror in Christ Jesus! Because of what Jesus did for you on the cross, all of these things are true! They describe the *real* you.

Citizens of a Heavenly Kingdom

As we have discussed, the whole concept of giving up one's "rights" to serve Christ can be very difficult to grasp for Americans and those from other democratic societies who have been taught from childhood to be independent and self-reliant. The common attitude is: "I will fight for my rights! I have a voice and my vote counts!"

Christian author and speaker John Bevere has written extensively about this concept. In my estimation, he has correctly stated that the Kingdom of God is not a democracy, but rather a monarchy with Jesus as our King. In monarchial forms of government, the subjects do not have any rights. What the king says is law. When we became Christians, we transferred our citizenship from the earthly kingdom to the heavenly one. We are now servants, even slaves, to the King of kings—Jesus Christ! We are to lay all of our rights and privileges at His feet. Our lives are His to do with it as He pleases. But what better life is there? He is love personified and wholly good.

Some of the greatest assets we enjoy as American citizens are our personal liberties and freedoms. It is unfortunate that they have also become some of our greatest obstacles when it comes to living for God. Do not get me wrong, I am proud and thankful to be an American; but it may be one of the reasons that transferring my identity to Christ from me has not been an easy process. Everything in our society is geared toward self. The American culture on the whole worships at the altar of self. If you do not believe this, look at the advertising campaigns that bombard you every day, slogans like:

"Because I am worth it!"

"Be all that you can be!"

"I did it my way!"

Who Am I?

Changing this mindset requires making a conscious decision. For you to ever reach your potential and fulfill your destiny, you must determine to literally transfer your identity to Christ from every other place. But why wouldn't you, especially when you understand that it is the path to the highest, most positive and fulfilling life possible?

A Helpful Exercise

Sometimes it helps to do something tangible to make an inward decision seem more official. Try this: Get a sheet of paper and a pen. Then set two chairs facing opposite each other. Sit in one chair while facing the empty one. The chair you are sitting in represents your present identity or the composite that makes up your identity. The empty chair represents Christ.

While you are seated, write down all of the labels you—and others—have used to describe yourself. Include both positive and negative attributes. Ask the Holy Spirit to reveal any labels you may not even be conscious of. Perhaps deep down you feel worthless, though you have never have voiced it or given it much thought. Sometimes the subconscious labels control us the most.

When you feel the list is complete and you are ready to release those labels, stand up, leaving your list in that chair. Then turn and sit down in the other chair. Your physical action will mirror the change taking place in your heart, the literal transference of your identity from yourself to Christ.

Many longtime believers and even many in the ministry have never really made this transfer of identity official. Yes, they are Christians who have made Jesus their Lord, but they have continued to rely on titles and labels to define themselves. Before you go on any further, why not take the time to do this exercise? It will serve as a demarcation line in your spiritual growth.

Process Follows Decision

Making the switch may begin with a quality decision, but allowing it to permeate every aspect of your life is a process. In my own situation, it has taken much time, prayer, and discipline; but it has changed my life completely. Every time I sense feelings of insecurity, I remind myself that *it is not I who live, but Christ Jesus who lives in me! I am a new person in Christ and my life is now hidden in Him!* Why do I do this? It is because *insecurity* is a fruit of *misplaced identity.*

Do you ever feel threatened when others are successful? Do you avoid certain places or people because of how uncomfortable and insecure you feel? Are you self-conscious? If so, it is likely that your identity has been misplaced. Think of it this way. When you are sick and the

symptoms are raging, you become very self-centered; your total focus is on getting better and rightfully so. On the other hand, when you are well, you rarely think about your physical health. You are free to focus on other things. Similarly, insecure people focus on themselves, but when they become secure in the Lord, firmly rooted in His love, they can easily take their eyes off of themselves and turn their attention toward other people.

You don't have to be controlled by negative attitudes and feelings. Jesus bore every insecurity you will ever experience, and He did this so that you could live free of them. Today can be a turning point in your life. Decide to go back to the situations that caused the insecurities in the first place, and with the help of the Holy Spirit you can begin to correct the problem from the root up.

Lord, forgive me for being so focused on myself and for relying on earthly labels to define me. I realize that my identity has been misplaced, but I am ready to change that. It is no longer I who live but Christ who lives in me and through me. Keep me mindful of this so that every form of insecurity will be replaced by confidence in who I am in Him. Amen.

CHAPTER 4

Get Real: The Role of Integrity

THE MOST IMPORTANT PART of a tree is the part hidden from view—the root system. This is where the tree receives the water and nutrients necessary to sustain life and that enable the tree to display its beauty above ground. It takes *healthy roots to produce healthy fruit.* As we have stated previously, the roots also provide the stability necessary for a tree to withstand all the storms that come against it. With each passing storm, the roots grow stronger.

The same is true for you. Once you establish a healthy foundation with your identity and security firmly rooted in Christ, much godly fruit will manifest in your life, an indication that the *Barnabas Factor* is operating in you. With each passing storm, or trial, your faith roots will only grow stronger. Your root system—the part of you that others do not see—will affect in a positive way the parts they do see, your actions and lifestyle.

The Tree Trunk

If the root system of the tree represents your identity and security, then the trunk represents *integrity*. Although externally the ground marks the point of distinction between the roots and the trunk, internally the two naturally "flow into" one another. The root system and the trunk play different roles, yet they are closely related. In fact you could say that their roles overlap where security is concerned. While the roots securely anchor the tree in the ground, the trunk provides added stability above ground. Integrity adds to the stability and security provided by a life firmly anchored in Christ.

Proverbs 10:9 clearly illustrates how closely security and integrity interrelate:

> The man of integrity walks securely, but he who takes crooked paths will be found out.

A person of integrity will walk securely, and a truly secure individual will be a person of integrity. In reality, you can't have one without the other.

Get Real: The Role of Integrity

A Good Example

Let me share a practical example to illustrate my point. Take the love walk, for instance. We understand that a believer is to exhibit the fruit of love, for it is the very nature of God. In order for this love to be like His love, however, it must be pure, free from ulterior motives. It cannot be selfish or manipulative, but totally unconditional. In other words, it must be a love based on the truth, or integrity. The only way a person can love others in this way, however, is for that individual to have a proper foundation in Christ. After all, Jesus said, "I am the truth." (John 14:6.) When a person's identity is found in Him, it is based upon Him who is the Truth—integrity personified.

By this we can conclude that integrity is one of the greatest blessings to flow from a healthy foundation based on Christ. In contemporary society, there is a great lack of integrity and moral clarity. This provides a great opportunity for the Church to shine. We as individual believers should lead the way toward integrity and right living. From the trunk of integrity will grow many wonderfully delicious fruits to meet the needs of people and whet the appetite of a world starved for the Truth. Living a life of integrity, with your roots firmly founded in Christ, will enable you to bear this fruit all of your days.

THE *Barnabas* FACTOR

Barnabas: A Man of Integrity

Barnabas is introduced to the readers of Acts by the following passage:

> Joseph, a Levite from Cyprus, whom the apostles called Barnabas (which means Son of Encouragement), sold a field he owned and brought the money and put it at the apostles' feet.
>
> Acts 4:36–37

From these two verses, we observe several things about Barnabas:

- He was a Levite, meaning that he was of the tribe that assisted the priests in the temple. This fact more than likely indicates that he was well schooled in the laws of the Old Testament.

- His home was Cyprus, an island in the Mediterranean Sea, where many Jews lived at that time.

- He was a landowner, which could indicate that he was wealthy.

- He was an encourager. Evidently *Barnabas* was a nickname for "Son of Encouragement." Think of that: this man was such an encourager that people changed his name to reflect it! I find it interesting that the Holy Spirit inspired the writer of Acts to introduce him in this way.

Get Real: The Role of Integrity

- He was a man of integrity. Now this fact is not evident at first glance, but a close examination of the verse will reveal this all-important quality.

Encouragement and integrity go hand-in-hand. In fact, true encouragement flows out of a heart of integrity. Before I explain any further, let me interject an important side note: I have observed that true encouragers in the Body of Christ have a strong sense of personal security; they know who they are in Christ. Because of this security, they are not threatened by those around them. They can, therefore, freely offer encouragement to others.

Encouragement versus Flattery

Encouragers should not be confused with those who flatter, however. *Flattery* is deceptive in nature and lacks integrity. It is self-centered in that the one who flatters usually wants something from the object of the adulation. Whether it is something as simple as the desire for affirmation or something as serious as manipulating an individual to do something unethical, flattery is diabolical in nature and should be avoided. Any form of manipulation is actually a form of witchcraft. When I sense a person flattering me, I ask God for discernment and make a mental note that the individual may not be trustworthy. I am not quick to believe the things this individual says without checking them out thoroughly.

Deception masked by flattery can be a hard thing to detect for two reasons. First, those who need strokes to affirm their own self-esteem eagerly listen to flattery, savoring every word. Identity based on anything other than Christ makes a person vulnerable. Secure individuals, on the other hand, are not easily duped. They are better equipped to avoid the cleverly disguised pitfalls that the enemy lays out for them. Secure people do not need the flattery of others to feel good about themselves. They simply need the affirmation of the Lord!

This is an issue that I had to deal with in my own life. What began in my childhood and adolescence as "Great game, Hal!" became "Great message, preacher!" as I entered the ministry. I'm not saying that all of those pats on the back were flattery, because I am sure many were sincere. The trap I had to learn to avoid, however, was deriving my self-worth and affirmation from these comments. If we look to others for our self-esteem, it puts us on a roller-coaster of emotions that will hold us captive. Our affirmation must come from the Father alone, because He is the only One capable of loving us unconditionally. Regardless of our successes or failures, He loves us with the same love all the time.

Today I receive compliments as a way to determine whether or not I have connected with my audience. They are no longer a validation of my self-worth because I have already been affirmed by God through His Son, Jesus Christ!

Get Real: the Role of Integrity

Some ministers scoff at compliments, thinking that doing this is a sign of humility. But I think of a compliment as a gift. To refuse a gift hurts the giver, so I advise others to receive compliments graciously. The next time someone gives you a compliment, look that individual in the eyes and sincerely thank them for it. It has been my experience that most believers are very sincere when they affirm others. The key is not to become dependent upon compliments or allow them to determine your value.

The second thing that makes it difficult to discern between flattery and true encouragement is being a flatterer oneself. Remember, a person will always reap what he or she sows. (Gal. 6:7–10.) If you sow truth, you will reap it. If, on the other hand, you sow deception, you will reap that. Flattery is actually a form of lying. With that in mind, consider what Proverbs 17:4 says: "Liars listen to liars" (GNT). Now I realize that is strong, but the principle is the same: flatterers listen to flatterers. Why? Because flattery has become a familiar spirit to them.

If, on the other hand, you are a person of integrity who always speaks the truth from a pure heart, you will easily discern whether or not someone else is operating in the spirit of truth. Deception will be a foreign spirit to you and you will recognize it as such. Always remember that it is "the little foxes that spoil the vine" (Song 2:15). It is the little habits that will build up over a lifetime and become either a blessing or a curse to you.

In this present age, discernment is very important for all believers. The Bible tells us that in the last days many will be deceived. Make sure you are sowing truth and integrity!

True Encouragement

We need more Barnabases in the Body of Christ today—men and women who are willing to encourage others from pure motives. *Encouragers* are those who come alongside and exhort the weary not to give up. They are the cheerleaders who urge us to keep going and to finish strong. Encouragers see the potential in others and have a way of drawing out the best in them. Their timely words are like oxygen to the soul.

I remember an instance from my high school days when I experienced this firsthand. I was running in a half-mile race. As I came out of the final turn and was heading for the finish line, I could feel myself running out of gas. I was in the lead, but I was growing weak and the other runners were closing in on me. All of a sudden, one of my friends came alongside me on the infield of the track and began to shout words of encouragement. It was as if he gave me a shot of adrenalin. His encouragement enabled me to put on the afterburners and cross the finish line in first place! He came along at just the right time!

Get Real: the Role of Integrity

This is a clear picture of what most of us need, true *encouragers* who will come alongside us and exhort us not to give up when the temptation is greatest. These encouragers are selfless individuals who are always looking for someone to build up.

This need is so critical that I would like you to pray with me now: "Father, please give us more true encouragers. Raise up people who are secure with who they are in Christ, who will stand alongside us in our weak moments, who will mentor us to success, and who will do it from a heart of purity and integrity! And, Father, make us encouragers too. Use us to speak a word in season to those who are weary. Amen."

The Truth, the Whole Truth, and Nothing but the Truth

We have established that Barnabas was known as "the Son of Encouragement" and that true encouragement can only come from a heart of integrity. But the writer of Acts gives us more evidence that Barnabas was a man of integrity. Although one might not see it at first glance, his actions prove it.

Once again, our text for this chapter states that Barnabas "sold a field he owned and brought the money and put it at the apostles' feet." Does that sound familiar to you? Perhaps you are more familiar with the land deal mentioned in the very next passage:

> Now a man named Ananias, together with his wife Sapphira, also sold a piece of property. With his wife's full knowledge he kept back part of the money for himself, but brought the rest and put it at the apostles' feet.
>
> Then Peter said, "Ananias, how is it that Satan has so filled your heart that you have lied to the Holy Spirit and have kept for yourself some of the money you received for the land? Didn't it belong to you before it was sold? And after it was sold, wasn't the money at your disposal? What made you think of doing such a thing? You have not lied to men but to God."
>
> When Ananias heard this, he fell down and died.
>
> Acts 5:1–5

Then, in verses 7–10, Sapphira fell prey to the exact same sin, resulting in the same outcome!

I believe that the writer of Acts was comparing the land sale of Barnabas (at the end of Acts 4) with that of Ananias and Sapphira (at the beginning of Acts 5). These two similar deals were handled in the complete opposite manner. Barnabas was governed by integrity, giving all of the money from his sale to the apostles. Ananias and Sapphira deceptively withheld some of the profit for themselves—a move that cost them their lives.

Get Real: The Role of Integrity

Integrity Defined

So what is *integrity* anyway? One meaning, that I heard years ago, is "the absence of folds." I like this definition because it is easy to illustrate using a white bed sheet. When a sheet is pulled tight over the surface of a mattress, there are no folds. It is completely flat with no shadows or hard-to-see places. If, in contrast, a sheet is merely tossed onto a bed, ripples and folds will be created that conceal parts of the sheet in darkness.

Integrity is "being singularly committed to a moral; it is the quality of being complete or undivided."[1] It is a quality used to describe someone who is wholly devoted to the Lord. There is no double-mindedness about whom this individual serves. Or, using the illustration of the bed sheet, there are no folds in this person's character, no shadowy dark places that hide sin. What you see is what you get. A person of integrity is pure inside and out.

Of people of integrity, Jesus said, "Blessed are the pure in heart, for they will see God" (Matt. 5:8). Purity of heart is no small matter in the eyes of God. Without it, we will not see Him! But with it, we will!

Reputation and Character: Two Different Things

I have heard it said that others know us by our reputation, by the things we have accomplished, by the way we act and treat others. Your image is what others perceive you to be based on what they see in your life. But God and the angels know us by the part of us that is unseen—our character, or lack of it. We all project an image for the world to see; but in your case, does that image match what you are really like in your thought life, who you are in your private moments?

Many years ago I heard this story, which illustrates my point:

> A young lawyer was sitting in his new office waiting for his first client. When he heard the door open, he quickly picked up the phone and tried to sound busy. The visitor could hear this young lawyer on the telephone saying, "Greg, I'll be flying to Boston on a new case; it looks like it's going to be a big one. When I get back, we need to talk to Steve about his Tulsa case. Greg, you'll have to excuse me, someone just came in. I'll be in touch."
>
> With that the attorney hung up. Turning to the man who had just entered, he said, "Now, how can I help you, sir?"
>
> With a big grin, the man replied, "I am from the telephone company, and I am here to hook up your phone."

If you choose to live your life with false pretenses, there will come a time when someone will come to "hook up your phone"! Deceptive sins will be exposed! Just ask Ananias and Sapphira. Integrity has no façades and knows no hypocrisy.

Get Real: The Role of Integrity

Pressure to Perform

There is an inherent "occupational hazard" for all believers, especially those in the ministry. People put Christians and spiritual leaders on a pedestal and expect them to act a certain way. This creates tremendous pressure for those on the pedestal to conform to that image. If the identity of these individuals is misplaced and they are insecure, they will likely give in to the pressure, their lives becoming more of a performance than a true reflection of who they are.

On the other hand, secure leaders are more concerned with projecting the image of Christ than trying to please others. They are people of integrity, true to who God has made them. Performing takes a great deal of energy, which could account for the amount of burnout so prevalent in the Church; but there is rest for the people whose identity is found in Christ. They are genuine, comfortable in their own skin. They remember that it is no longer they who live, but Christ who lives through them. (Gal. 2:20.)

It is also tempting for believers to project the image that everything is great in their lives. Many fear they will be judged as weak Christians if people find out that they have problems. The sad thing is that doing this isolates hurting individuals when they need interaction with others the most! Besides, the Scripture clearly says that "a righteous man may have many troubles" (Ps. 34:19). All of us encounter difficulties from time to time, but the good news is, He promises to deliver us out of them all! This is not to say that you wear the pain on your sleeves for all the world to see; but if you will ask Him, God will lead you to genuinely caring individuals, true encouragers who will stand with you in your hour of need.

I believe this pressure to act a certain way and put forth a flawless image is a result of the Church becoming performance driven. Often the emphasis is on *doing* rather than *being*, which is no different from the value system of the world. God, on the other hand, is more interested in who you are than in all the great things you can do for Him. What we *do* in our Christian walk is supposed to flow out of who we *are* as a result of His grace. Our lives are merely to reflect His. Another way of saying this is that our Christian walk and our ministries must come out of the overflow of our relationship with Jesus. Next we will explore this relationship in depth.

> *Lord, as I grow in my understanding of the real me, help me to be true to that image. I don't want my life to be merely a performance to fulfill others' expectations. You are the only One I want to please. When I'm hurting, lead me to encouragers with whom I can "be real." Then help me to be a person of integrity, an encourager instead of a flatterer, a person whose word is always good, someone others can rely upon. I want to be pure through and through, just like You. Amen.*

CHAPTER 5

Get Vertical!

IN RECENT YEARS, Mountain Dew, a popular soft drink in the United States, had an ad slogan that said, "Get vertical!" It gave the impression that if you drank their drink, you would have the energy to really enjoy life and take part in exciting adventures. It is a well-known fact, however, that the zip in Mountain Dew can be attributed to its large concentration of caffeine. You will "get vertical" all right, and you might *stay vertical* all night long if you drink too much!

We believers need to "get vertical" every day. No, I am not advocating that you drink a can of Mountain Dew every morning. I am referring to the vertical relationship we need with Jesus. With our busy lives, it is a challenge to set aside this time on a daily basis, but when we do, we will then be better equipped to tackle the adventures of life and truly be able to enjoy them!

This brings us to back to something else that is vertical—the tree we have been using as our analogy of the believer. I do not think it is a coincidence that God chose to compare us to trees that reach heavenward for the sunlight. We, too, reach heavenward toward the Son, the light of the world. This vertical relationship is the cry of every believer's heart, and that is what we will focus on now.

So far, we have discussed the importance of the root system and the trunk of the tree—identity, security, and integrity. Building upon this foundation, I would like to share a key observation I have made after years of pondering these things. I began to notice that the Christians that I knew who were secure, solid people of integrity, had one thing in common—a fresh, vibrant, "vertical" relationship with Jesus. They were not overburdened and downcast, but full of joy and life. The *Barnabas Factor* is a natural by-product of those who keep their relationship with Jesus fresh!

These believers, whose enthusiasm for God is contagious, serve Him not because they have to but because they want to follow Him. Simply put, they have discovered that "to know Him is to love Him." This type of love relationship is what being a follower of Christ is all about. True

Christianity isn't a religion based upon a code of ethics or an endless string of do's and don'ts. It is a love relationship with the living Son of God.

What Is the Reason?

As believers, why then should we strive to be holy or live lives of integrity? Is it because of the Ten Commandments or because our church leaders have told us to do so? No, our primary motivation is not supposed to come from external pressure; it is to flow freely from within. Our motivation should be because we love Jesus and want to please Him! It's that simple.

Take the example of my relationship with my wife. Why do I do thoughtful things for her? Why do I take my role as her husband seriously and do my best to serve and protect her? Nobody has to tell me to do these things. I just do them. Why? Because I love her! The creative ways in which I demonstrate my love for Lisa flow freely out of my love for her. She is such a wonderful lady; it is easy to stay motivated.

It is supposed to be the same way in our relationship with Jesus. Our daily Christian walk (our *doing*) should be an overflow of our love relationship with Him (our *being*). The Ten Commandments are to be a standard, or a measuring stick, by which we can gauge how we are doing in our love walk, for example. In the Old Testament God wrote His

Law on tablets of stone, but now He writes them on our hearts. (See Jer. 31:33.) This is a sign of relationship.

If our motives are truly from a heart of love for Jesus, then we will never become religious or out of touch with what the Spirit of God is doing in the world today. Believers who understand this simple truth are the most fruitful in the Kingdom, and I believe that at the end of their days, they will hear the words, "Well done, good and faithful servant" (Matt. 25:21). Why? It is because all their good deeds stem from a relationship with the Lord instead of being dead works wrought by the arm of the flesh.

Location, Location, Location

The Psalmist used the analogy of trees to describe the types of believers who have this kind of delightful relationship with the Lord:

> They are like trees planted along the riverbank,
>   bearing fruit each season.
> Their leaves never wither,
>   and they prosper in all they do.
>
>   Psalm 1:3 NLT

Here it is the *location* of the trees that is of prime importance. I cannot emphasize this enough! We must be planted by the River of Life from which flow all the blessings needed

to sustain us spiritually. Another way of saying this is that we must have a fresh relationship with Jesus.

We cannot live in the Spirit without this vital connection. If you remove yourself from this Source of life-giving water, one of two things will happen. You will either begin to operate out of a religious spirit of legalism—resulting in works of the flesh—or you will simply backslide, which begs the question: *where are you planted?*

For years, when I would read about the trees mentioned in Psalm 1, I thought of them in the context of where I grew up, in the hills of West Virginia. There the landscape is covered with green, lush trees whether they are located beside a stream or not. Abundant rainfall makes water plentiful throughout the countryside.

The context for this Psalm, however, is Israel, where the climate is quite different. There it is arid and not much grows unless it is in close proximity to a stream or other water source. If you were to remove a tree from the banks of a river in Israel and plant it in the middle of a field, it would eventually wither and die. Apart from the river, the land simply cannot sustain the life of a tree.

Fruitful believers stay planted by the River of Life, partaking of its refreshment day after day. They don't rely on a drink they had last week and allow themselves to become parched, but they draw daily. As Jesus said, "Whoever drinks the water I give him will never thirst" (John 4:14).

The Trap of Legalism

Constantly partaking of this living water will also prevent us from falling into the trap of legalism, like so many well-meaning believers. Let me give you an example from my own life. I have made the personal decision not to drink alcohol. The issue here is *why*. Is it a legalistic mandate that has been legislated to me by others in the Church? No, I do not drink because of my love relationship with Jesus.

Let me explain. I realize that my body is the temple of the Holy Spirit and I do not want to put anything in my body that could potentially hinder me in any way. Alcohol can impair my senses. It could be used by the devil to trap me in addiction. It is expensive, and there are better uses for my finances. I have witnessed youth in the church struggle with addiction. In the beginning these young people justified drinking with their buddies because their parents drank socially. Whether we want to admit it or not, everything we do affects the people around us, and I do not want to cause anyone to stumble. This conviction has come out of my daily relationship with the Lord, and I know it would grieve Him if I were to override it.

Now, if you feel that the Lord approves of you drinking alcohol, it is between the two of you. Each person must live according to his or her own conscience. I would, however, encourage you to examine your motives. Is your greatest

desire to please the Lord? Is your desire to drink merely to protest the legalism that you have seen in the Church? Are you trying to display your "freedom in Christ"?

Some think that "freedom in the Spirit" means that they can be social drinkers and not feel guilty, but that is actually the opposite of legalism. It is what theologians call *antinomianism*, which simply means, "no laws."[2] True "freedom in the Spirit" is being free to do those things that please the Lord as well as being free *not* do those things that displease Him.

Even though my conviction has come as a result of my relationship with Jesus, if I were to neglect that relationship and allow it to grow stagnant, I could easily slip into a legalistic attitude. I might begin to expect others to adhere to the same values I live by and become judgmental of those who reject them. Legalism—the letter of the law—produces death. I believe it is why we see so many believers who have a form of godliness but are not walking in the power Jesus has made available to us. (See 2 Tim. 3:5.)

There is a fine line between legalism and lawlessness, and we must be careful not to slip into either ditch. Life in the Spirit is the narrow road, which avoids either extreme. It is where we receive the power necessary to live a victorious, joy-filled Christian life. The only way to walk it is through a daily relationship with Jesus. There is simply no other way.

Peter Deyneka—a famous missionary from the nineteenth century and founder of the Slavic Gospel Association—once wrote: "Much prayer much power!" I think that sums it up well. Prayer is simply communication with God, and it is through our moment-by-moment conversation with Him that we are able to walk in the Spirit and partake of His power.

Lack of Prayer, Devastating Consequences

The scene in the Garden of Gethsemane illustrates the challenge that often accompanies prayer. If you will recall, Jesus was well aware that His time to bear our sin was soon approaching. He knew He needed an extended time with the Father and had requested that His closest friends—Peter, James, and John—sit up with Him while He prayed. Jesus went a short distance away from the disciples, and when he returned the first time and found them sleeping, He said, "Simon, … are you asleep? Could you not keep watch for one hour? Watch and pray so that you will not fall into temptation. The spirit is willing, but the body is weak" (Mark 14:37–38).

The scene portrays the very human side of the disciples. Does this scene hit close to home for you? I certainly can relate to it. For years, I struggled with the temptation to get a few more minutes of sleep rather than rising early to begin my day in prayer. The Lord knew that my desire was to get up and pray, but my flesh would win the internal struggle more times than not. After I would get up, I would feel guilty that I had not gotten up earlier to pray.

Because of the disciples' lack of prayer, they had no clue as to what was about to take place and were, in effect, left to deal with the situation on their own. We, of course, know the devastating consequence this had on Peter who was not able to withstand the temptation to deny Christ. All of their lives were thrown into turmoil and they were not prepared. Perhaps if these men had been seeking God at the same time Jesus was, they might have received wisdom and strength to deal with the events in a more positive way.

No Heavenly Time Clock

Slumber is enemy *numero uno* for prayer. We must all conquer this fruit of the flesh if we are going to enjoy victory in our lives on a consistent basis. Please understand me, I am not saying that you have to spend one hour in prayer every day in order to have God's power present in your life. He does not have a heavenly time clock that must be punched every day. The point of prayer is to nurture your relationship with Jesus, not to perform a religious exercise. Spending "one hour in prayer" is a guideline. We are to follow the *spirit* of the law, not the *letter* of the law.

When Lisa and I go out for a date, we generally spend about an hour enjoying a meal together. During this time we may talk about a variety of things. Sometimes the conversation is upbeat and lighthearted. Other times there may be a more serious tone. The point is, we do not set a timer on the length of our conversation, nor do we have a strict set of guidelines as to what we talk about. We "go with the flow," so to speak, and that is the way our prayer time is to be.

As we develop our relationship with Jesus, we learn to sense when the "conversation" is over and when it is to go to action. On some occasions the prayer time may be shorter than an hour and other times it will be much longer.

You might be thinking, *How can I get to the point that I truly desire to spend this kind of time in the presence of the Lord?* For me I simply asked for that desire. I prayed that God would place a yearning in my heart to spend time with Him every day, and you know what? He answered my request! He will do the same for you.

Love: The Great Motivator

Have you ever noticed the transformation of a young man in love? It is amazing. Suddenly, although he has never had the slightest interest in reading love poems, he now begins *writing* them for his new love. It is as though this romantic love has enabled him to tap into a previously unknown reservoir of creative ability. He buys flowers and gifts. This guy who used to sleep until noon now rises early

just to be with his girl, never uttering one word of complaint. He is always smiling and thinking about ways to demonstrate his love to her. Needless to say, he is motivated. Perhaps you have experienced this phenomenon firsthand. Whether you have been the pursuer or the one pursued, you know it is a life-changing experience that brings out the best in you.

The point is, a young man in love is motivated internally, not externally. He *can't wait* to do these things, and that is our goal in our love relationship with Jesus! We are to pursue Him with every fiber of our being. After all He is pursuing us with the same fervor!

Perhaps you have experienced this kind of relationship with the Lord in the past, but now the desire has cooled. You are still serving Him, but the life seems to have gone out of your relationship. Maybe you can relate to those in the church at Ephesus whom Jesus addressed:

> "I know your deeds, your hard work and your perseverance. I know that you cannot tolerate wicked men, that you have tested those who claim to be apostles but are not, and have found them false. You have persevered and have endured hardships for my name, and have not grown weary."
>
> Revelation 2:2–3

These were good people who did great works. They were holy and did not tolerate sin in their lives or in the lives of other believers. Jesus was pleased with them and commended them. Yet, something was missing, which He reveals in the next verses:

> "Yet I hold this against you: You have forsaken your first love. Remember the height from which you have fallen! Repent and do the things you did at first. If you do not repent, I will come to you and remove your lampstand from its place."
>
> vv. 4–5

These believers had moved away from the Source. Their works were no longer an overflow of a love relationship with Jesus, but rather they had slipped into the arena of dead works. This is a dangerous place to be, based on His warning.

Rekindle the Flame

Reminiscent of advice given to married couples who have lost their first love, Jesus gives the Ephesian believers a remedy to correct their condition. He counsels them do again the things they did when their love for Him was first kindled.

Remember how you felt when you were first born again? The world was bright, clean, and you loved everyone! You were so eager to learn that you were like a dry sponge soaking up every drop of water around. Life was wonderful! The emotions are very similar for a newlywed couple. In both cases, those strong feelings can begin to cool as life together becomes routine.

In order for husbands and wives to rekindle their flame, it is helpful for them to remember the things that initially attracted them to one another. Focusing on those qualities often sparks renewed passion and fresh water begins to spring up in wells that had run dry.

Likewise, by remembering why you chose to give your life to Jesus in the first place, a smoldering ember will once again become a flaming fire. A spiritual well that has been dry for years will once again spring to life as living water begins to flow. Dry religiosity will give way to an unquenchable zeal for God.

The words of Sue McBeth—a nineteenth-century missionary to North American Indians—sum it up well: "First, and most important: Go to your work directly from your knees. Do not leave your [prayer] closet until you feel that God is with you, by His Spirit." What a timely and pertinent exhortation!

Semper Paratus

Some may accuse me of having a religious spirit for saying that we must spend time in prayer every day in order to have God's power at work in our lives. Think of it in terms of the military. Try telling the U.S. Marines or the U.S. Navy SEALS that they do not need to prepare for their combat missions. How successful would they be if they only showed up occasionally for training and then were told to report for duty!

Why have the Navy SEALS not lost many soldiers in combat? The reason is simple: they train and prepare continually! The U.S. Coast Guard's motto is: *Semper Paratus*, which means, "Always Prepared." Sounds like an excellent motto for believers as well. How do we prepare for the battles of everyday life? We can only do it through prayer, worship, and study of the Word on a daily basis. It is the only way to keep the flames of our first love for Jesus burning brightly. Just like having a good marriage and becoming an excellent soldier take work and discipline, so does developing our relationship with the Lord.

Relationship and Motivation

Returning to our narrative in Acts 4 and 5, there is an important lesson to learn about the motivation of our hearts. I believe Barnabas gave all the money from his land sale to the apostles for two reasons: because He loved God and, I believe, because he was obeying what the Father had led him to do. This act was sincere and reflected who he was. I do not believe he did it so that others would think he was a great man—to polish his image; nor do I believe it was because the leaders had pressured him. Furthermore, I do not believe his gift was based on a legalistic interpretation of

the Scripture. I believe Barnabas was motivated by the fresh, vibrant, vertical relationship he shared with His Lord.

Ananias and Sapphira, on the other hand, were all about image. They gave the money from their land sale deceptively, keeping some of it back for themselves. What others thought of them was more important than being open and honest. They were more interested in pleasing people and indulging their greed than pleasing the Father. This was a sign that they had moved away from the Source even though they were in the midst of a tremendous revival.

No matter what is going on around us, we must *never* neglect our daily, personal time with Jesus! Powerful church services are good, but they can never replace one-on-one time with Him. This is, in my opinion, why many believers burn out after great revivals. They rely on the "goose-bump" feelings to get them through life, but that is like building a house on sand; there is nothing sturdy to anchor them. But those who enjoy the revival while maintaining their personal relationship with the Lord build on an unshakeable foundation and are motivated by pure hearts.

Telling Moments

Joseph, from the Old Testament, provides another look at the power of relationship. Why do you think he was able to continually resist the sexual advances of Potiphar's wife, even though he probably could have gotten away with having an ongoing, torrid affair? Think about it: he was far from home. As Mrs. Potiphar's slave, Joseph was her property and he could have claimed that he was just "following orders." Furthermore, they were living in a culture that did not necessarily frown on such a lifestyle. (See Genesis 39:6–10.)

Do you think Joseph could have resisted her advances if he had made a habit of thinking about being with beautiful women or had even contemplated submitting to her advances? Of course not!

Joseph's choice to run was a result of an affair of a different sort, an affair of the heart. He had spent his life meditating on God's Word. His ability to flee temptation naturally flowed from the love relationship he had with his Father. How can I so confidently make that assertion? Look at Joseph's initial response to Mrs. Potiphar's seductive advances? "How could I do such a wicked thing? It would be a great sin against God" (v. 9 NLT). Joseph would not violate his relationship with his Lord. Whatever is on the inside of a person will come out in times of pressure!

Jesus was in an even greater press in the Garden of Gethsemane. It was His greatest moment of temptation and all of eternity rested on His shoulders. How did He respond? In deep anguish, with sweat falling to the ground as drops of blood, He declared to His Father, "Not my will, but yours be done" (Luke 22:42). That pivotal, monumental decision was preceded by a lifetime of obedience to the Father, even in the

little things. Jesus had nurtured His relationship with the Father, never neglecting it, regardless of the demands and busyness of the ministry. Based upon His integrity and desire to please His Father, there was only one decision Jesus could make and it was the right one.

So how about you? Where is your tree planted? Are you firmly planted by the living water through an ongoing, vibrant relationship with Jesus?

The prophet Jeremiah describes the rewards of such a life:

"Blessed are those who trust in the LORD
and have made the LORD their hope and confidence.
They are like trees planted along a riverbank,
with roots that reach deep into the water.
Such trees are not bothered by the heat
or worried by long months of drought.
Their leaves stay green,
and they never stop producing fruit."

Jeremiah 17:7–8 NLT

Next we will take a look at this fruit. When we are planted by the living water through our relationship with Jesus, it will come forth in abundance. Not only will we benefit personally, but this fruit will be a great blessing to all of the people we touch every day.

Lord, the greatest cry of my heart is to truly know You, to share a vital relationship with you every single day. You know that my spirit is willing but my flesh is often weak.

Help me to be more disciplined. Increase my hunger and thirst for righteousness that I may seek You with my whole heart. Quench my thirst with Your living water and satisfy my hunger with the milk and meat of Your Word. Amen.

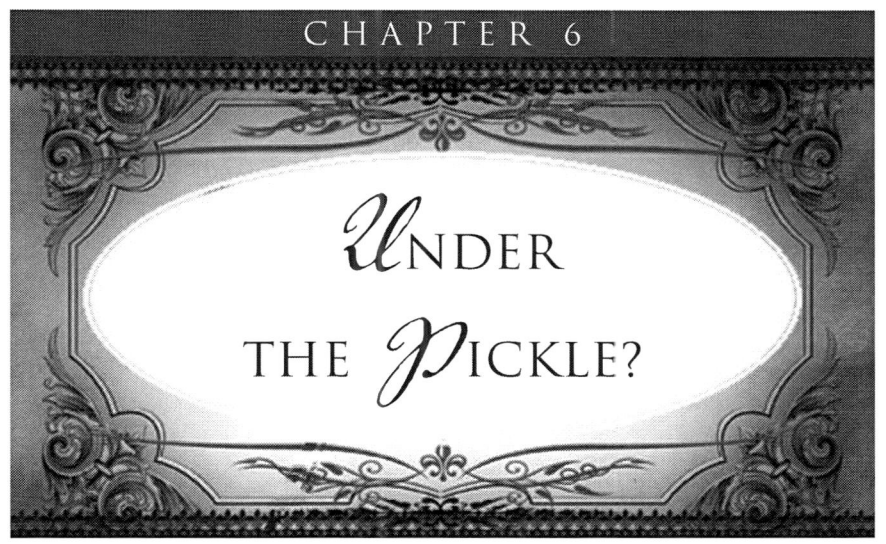

CHAPTER 6

Under the Pickle?

MANY YEARS AGO, the Wendy's Corporation ran an ad campaign that highlighted the generous size of their hamburger patties. Of their competitors they asked the question: "Where's the beef?" The answer was, "Under the pickle!" This illustrated that the beef from other fast-food restaurants was so small that it was hidden by a single pickle chip!

With this in mind, I think it is a fair question to ask believers, "Where's the *fruit?*"

Sadly for many, the answer may be: "Hidden by my insecurities!"

The quality of any fruit is determined by the health of the tree. If the root system is receiving the proper nourishment and the tree is firmly anchored and strong, likely the fruit of that tree will be delicious and abundant, an indication of the *Barnabas Factor* at work. If not, the crop will be inferior or possibly void of fruit altogether!

For Christians, the amount of fruit, its quality, and the longevity with which we bear it is determined in much the same way. Are we healthy believers with our identity correctly rooted in Christ? Are we receiving the proper nourishment by partaking daily of living water? Or are we plagued with insecurities because our identity is rooted in some other place? Are our food and water tainted with toxins?

The apostle Paul instructed wisely:

> Now, just as you accepted Christ Jesus as your Lord, you must continue to live in obedience to him. Let your *roots grow down into him and draw up nourishment from him*, so you will grow in faith, strong and vigorous in the truth you were taught.
>
> Colossians 2:6 NLT (96, emphasis added)

When we are healthy and whole, we can experience the blessings described in Psalm 92:

> The righteous will flourish like a palm tree,
>   they will grow like a cedar of Lebanon;
> planted in the house of the LORD,

Under the Pickle?

they will flourish in the courts of our God.
They will still bear fruit in old age,
they will stay fresh and green,
proclaiming, "The LORD is upright;
he is my Rock, and there is no wickedness in him."

vv. 12–15

We can expect to flourish, even in our old age! We will bear fruit and be full of strength and life, able to proclaim the faithfulness of the Lord for a sustained period of time!

The Reverend Billy Graham is an excellent example of this. Not only has his ministry been fruitful for over sixty years, throughout it all he has been one of the most respected individuals of our time. Why, out of all the spiritual leaders in our nation, has Billy Graham's counsel been sought so often by United States presidents? Why is he, even in old age, still being asked to pray at presidential inaugurations? It is because he is a man of unquestionable integrity. As the passage above describes, "There is no wickedness in him." May the same be said of us.

Always remember this: *Others do not remember how fast we start. They only remember how strong we finish!* Let us determine to finish strong, our lives flourishing with abundant fruit.

Horizontal Relationship

Once again, our location is a crucial element in our development. In the last chapter we discussed the importance of being planted by the streams of living water through our vertical relationship with Jesus. It is equally important that we be "planted in the house of the LORD," the local church. It is there that we develop our *horizontal* relationships. Through them we receive additional "nutrients" critical to our health. The writer of Hebrews understood this:

> Let us not give up meeting together, as some are in the habit of doing, but let us encourage one another—and all the more as you see the Day approaching.
>
> Hebrews 10:25

The encouragement of other believers is essential to our spiritual health. The apostle Peter warned that our enemy, the devil, "prowls around like a roaring lion looking for someone to devour" (1 Peter 5:8). How do lions attack? They seek the weak and vulnerable, the stragglers who are alone and not alert. The quickest way to be attacked by the enemy is to remove yourself from the fellowship of other believers. Isolation is a dangerous place. May this word to the wise be sufficient for us. We cannot control all of the difficulties that come against us, but God's Word clearly lays out the things that we *can* do to ensure that we overcome. Staying plugged into the local church is key.

The focus of this chapter is the connection between the local church and the *fruit* that we can expect to bear as we become planted there. To understand this, we will again examine the life of Barnabas. It is certain that no one ever asked of him, "Where's the fruit?"

Understand the Setting

Before we delve into this, however, it might be interesting and helpful for you to understand the overall setting at the time. Prior to the outbreak of the Antioch revival, Jesus had spoken the following words before He ascended into heaven:

> "You will receive power when the Holy Spirit comes on you; and you will be my witnesses in *Jerusalem*, and in all *Judea* and *Samaria*, and *to the ends of the earth*."
>
> Acts 1:8 (emphasis added)

I believe He actually outlined the book of Acts with that statement, which you can see by the following breakdown:

- Acts 1–7   The Church was first established in *Jerusalem* and *Judea*.
- Acts 8   Philip the evangelist then took the message to the *Samaritans*.
- Acts 10   Peter began the process of taking the Gospel *"to the ends of the earth"* when

he entered Cornelius' home and preached the Good News there among the Gentiles.

- Acts 11–28   The remainder of Acts chronicles the spreading of the Gospel throughout the known world.

At the time that Peter was explaining to the church at Jerusalem why he had preached the Gospel to the Gentiles at Cornelius' house, the revival at Antioch, which we discussed in chapter 2, was also taking place. To refresh your memory, there the Holy Spirit was working through some courageous believers from Cyrene in North Africa and from Cyprus, an island on the eastern side of the Mediterranean. Through them the Good News of Jesus Christ was spread to the Gentiles in Antioch and ultimately around the world.

It is interesting to note that even though both Cornelius and the converts at Antioch were Gentiles, there was a difference. Cornelius, a proselyte, was at least an observer of the Jewish law and a worshiper of God. The Gentiles in Antioch, on the other hand, were totally pagan before the early missionaries introduced them to Jesus. That is where we will pick up our narrative.

Under the Pickle?

Whom Shall We Send?

> Now those who had been scattered by the persecution in connection with Stephen traveled as far as Phoenicia, Cyprus and Antioch, telling the message only to Jews. Some of them, however, men from Cyprus and Cyrene, went to Antioch and began to speak to Greeks also, telling them the good news about the Lord Jesus. The Lord's hand was with them, and a great number of people believed and turned to the Lord.
>
> Acts 11:19–21

The winds of missions were beginning to blow in full force, and the world would never be the same. Naturally, workers were needed to help with the multitude of new converts from this revival. (Or, as I like to call it, a great "*vi*-val." Since this was the first time the Gospel had reached these people, there was nothing to "*re*-vive".) Do you recall from earlier who was sent to the local church at Antioch?

> News of this reached the ears of the church at Jerusalem, and they sent Barnabas to Antioch.
>
> v. 22

Of all the people in the early Church, why did they send Barnabas? One reason might be that since Barnabas was originally from Cyprus, he more than likely would have known the believers from there who had gone to evangelize Antioch. These believers would no doubt have felt comfortable with him especially if a situation arose—a doctrinal issue, for example—during the revival that required correction.

It also shows that the early Church leaders had great faith and confidence in Barnabas. They were certain that he would not only know what to do, but that he would handle it well. In chapter 2 we saw that Barnabas was a very secure individual. Apparently this enabled others to have confidence in him as well.

Walls of Prejudice

> When [Barnabas] arrived [at Antioch] and saw the evidence of the grace of God, he was glad and encouraged them all [Jews and Gentiles] to remain true to the Lord with all their hearts.
>
> v. 23

At face value, this verse does not appear to be that significant, other than the fact that Barnabas encouraged the believers to remain true to the Lord. Considering the culture at the time this was written, however, there are important aspects that would be easily missed if we were only to view this verse through contemporary lenses. First, it is important to remember that prior to his conversion, Barnabas had been a practicing Jewish man. Today, we would refer to him as an Orthodox Jew. In other words, he took his faith seriously.

Second, it is also important to understand that Jewish converts in the early Church still observed many of the Jewish laws and customs that they always had, which means that they also retained their prejudices. What is significant about that here is that the Jews were extremely intolerant of Gentiles. They were, in fact, so prejudiced that the first-century Jews called them "dogs," believing them to be no more worthy to receive the blessing of Abraham than dogs!

The point here is that it is quite amazing that Barnabas—considering his cultural background—could witness this explosive growth of *Gentile* converts and be glad about it! Instead of becoming entrenched in a "religious" mentality and rejecting this new thing, he embraced it and encouraged these believers to remain true to the Lord with all their hearts.

A Side Note

It is a sad commentary that, long before Jesus arrived, the Jews referred to those outside their culture as "dogs." Apparently they had forgotten that God had set Israel apart to be a nation of missionaries.

> Darkness as black as night will cover all the nations of the earth,
> but the glory of the Lord will shine over you.

All nations will come to your light;
mighty kings will come to see your radiance.

Isaiah 60:2–3 NLT

Does that sound familiar? Sad to say, many in the Church today have a similar opinion concerning reaching the lost around the world. They may know better than to call the unsaved "dogs," but their lack of action speaks differently. You know what? God's plan has not changed! His people are still called to be a light unto the nations.

The Dreaded Beast of Change

Thankfully, Barnabas let go of his prejudices and embraced the Gentiles, which brings up an essential fruit of a life rooted in Christ's identity—being willing to change as the Holy Spirit leads. Barnabas was not married to traditions, stale patterns, and old habits; rather he was united to Christ. Unlike some religious leaders who passionately despise change, his heart was open and pliable before the Lord. He was able to "think outside of the box" and be open to God working in new ways.

It is common to hear Christians say, "Well, it has never been done like that around here." By giving place to this type of attitude, believers unwittingly limit themselves to only what has already been done before. They cannot see beyond that and believe God for greater things, new things.

Under the Pickle?

A religious attitude coupled with a poverty mentality will create a very narrow view of the world, shutting down vision and the move of God quicker than a hungry dog goes after a ham bone.

I believe this limited mindset is one of the reasons so many believers are walking in defeat today. They have unconsciously subscribed to insanity—doing the same thing over and over again but expecting a different result. Because of many believers' unwillingness to change, they keep marching around the same mountain, hoping that God will somehow answer their prayers, when God is all the while saying, "Stop walking around that mountain. It is time to head north and take the Promised Land!" (Deut. 2:3.) In other words, do something different. Go a different way because what you are doing now is not working!

How about you? Do you feel like you are going around in circles, not receiving the answers to your prayers? Why not prayerfully examine what you are doing and ask the Father if you need to change course.

Some Things Will Never Change

Another mistake many in the Church make concerning change is that they confuse things that *can* change with those things that can *never* change. Allow me to explain. In the Christian faith, there are what I call *nonnegotiable essentials*, components that can never change. The message of salvation by faith in Christ alone is one example. There is only one way to the Father and that will never change regardless of time, location, or any other factor. Another example is the Word of God. The Scriptures are sacred, inspired by the Holy Spirit, and without error. These two things are essential to our faith. They cannot nor will they ever change. They are etched in stone, if you will.

There are, however, aspects of the Christian faith that can change, such as the *methods* that are used to share the Gospel. The message is unchanging, but the methods may vary from generation to generation and culture to culture. Many missionaries have found out the hard way that what may work in their home country may not work *at all* on foreign soil. The local culture must be taken into consideration if one is to reach the people of that area.

Who would have dreamed, for example, several generations ago that the *Jesus* film and the *Passion of the Christ* would prove to be the greatest evangelistic tools ever used to share the Gospel of Jesus Christ with the world? Billions have seen the life of Christ and heard His message on the big screen.

The *message* has not changed—but thanks to advances in technology and gifted writers and actors, we have gained powerful new *methods* to make the Good News known. Just think what the world would have missed out on had these creative individuals been stuck in the past, married to

outdated methods! But because of God-inspired innovations, countless millions have experienced Jesus' love that might not have any other way. It is no secret that Hollywood has abused the medium, but that is no reason to condemn the tool and throw the baby out with the bathwater. God put the technology in the mind of man to be used for His glory.

Another example of changing methods is in the realm of *worship music.* I believe, for example, that the pipe organ is a wonderful instrument. For centuries God's people enjoyed singing hymns played on them. Today, however, it is much more common for this type of music to be played on guitars, keyboards, and drums. The styles of music have changed over the years as have the instruments used to play them; nevertheless, if the music lifts up the name of Jesus and exalts our great God, it is still worship music.

Why then, do some insist on using archaic methods to reach our contemporary culture? Is there a legitimate reason that we should only use styles and instruments that were created hundreds of years ago before electricity was even discovered? No, God is a contemporary God who knows how to speak effectively to our culture through the forms that are most meaningful to us. There are some who still prefer the pipe organ, but on the whole, today's generation enjoys worship music played on an electronic keyboard or a standard piano. The bottom line is, which is more effective in ministering to the target audience?

In the area of missions, this is called *contextualization*. In other words, put the message in the local context, so the people in that context can understand it. Those who resist this methodology are confusing what can never change with those elements of the Christian faith that are not set in stone. The *message* can never be tampered with, but the *methods* are endless. Those who cannot change run the risk of trying to reach an MP3 generation with 8-track tapes. Talk about being out of touch!

Speed Boats versus Ocean Liners

Having said that, I have observed that in general, the older people become, the more resistant to change they are. This is why young people are often more open to the leading of the Holy Spirit than some of their elders. Because they are open to change, youth are seen at the forefront of nearly every revival. Meanwhile, many of the older generation hang back and shake their heads, saying things like, "I'm not too sure about this. I haven't ever seen anything like it before."

Young people can be likened to tiny speed boats, which can quickly turn without much notice. Older folks are more like ocean liners, which require a much greater berth—several miles in some instances—to make a turn. Because of this tendency, the older we become, the more careful we must be not to lose our sense of adventure or our willingness to take risks and do whatever the Lord leads, no matter how unconventional it is.

The Curse of Solomon

I call the tendency to get stuck in the past and to be skeptical of change the Curse of Solomon. Like many believers, King Solomon was faithful and devoted to the Lord as a young man. His relationship with God was vibrant and alive. God even appeared to him and offered him whatever he wanted. Because Solomon's heart was so pure, he only asked for wisdom to lead God's people effectively. In other words, he was saying, "Lord, I just want to be obedient to Your call!" (See 2 Chron. 1:7–12.)

Sadly, like so many believers, over time Solomon let his relationship with God slip. His faith began to wane and his heart grew cold because his life was no longer rooted in the Source. How did it happen? It is possible that he became so involved in the work of the Lord that he forgot to spend time nurturing his relationship with Him. It is easy for us to fall into that trap today, if we are not careful. "Preventative maintenance" is required. As we discussed in the previous chapter, relationships require constant cultivation for them to thrive. In Solomon's case, he fell so far away that at the end of his days he concluded, "'Meaningless! Meaningless!' says the Teacher. 'Utterly meaningless! Everything is meaningless'" (Eccl. 1:2). I have seen far too many longtime believers fall prey to this curse and either burn out; backslide; or grow cold, religious, and resistant to change. Let this not be said of us! Let Solomon's example serve as a sufficient warning to us to keep our relationship with God close and personal.

The Pharisees and the teachers of the Law at the time of Christ were the epitome of those resistant to change. Totally mired in the Law and their traditions, they despised change so much that they did everything in their power to stop it, ultimately consenting to crucify Jesus! The "new thing" that God was doing in the earth through Him was too radical for them to accept. But thank God, there were and always have been those willing to follow Him at all cost, those willing to adapt to what the Holy Spirit is doing at any given time. I, for one, am committed to being one of those. I do not want to miss one thing that God is doing in the earth.

Prejudiced Spirit

Thank the Lord that Barnabas did not resist change; rather he exhibited the true Spirit of Christ and gladly embraced the new thing God was doing through the Gentiles. Rather than allowing racial and cultural prejudice to control him, Barnabas yielded to the fruit of love that had been shed abroad in his heart by the Holy Spirit. (Rom. 5:5.)

Under the Pickle?

Show me a man or a woman who is prejudiced toward others—whether it is due to race, gender, nationality, denominational affiliation, social status, economic level, or any other factor—and I will show you an insecure person whose identity is *not* rooted in Christ and whose heart is void of God's love! It is sad that two thousand years after Barnabas overcame this obstacle, many in the Church today are still grappling with this issue. Oh, how it must grieve the heart of God who loves us all equally.

As I have shared, for me, the identity issue was settled some time ago—first and foremost, I am a Christian. Any other label used to describe me—such as my gender, nationality, race, marital status, or profession—is secondary to who I am in Christ. I take a similar approach in relation to others. First and foremost I see all people as having value because they are created in the image of God, whether they are believers or not. When it comes to believers, I view them as Christians first. Any other quality or characteristic attached to them is secondary. When the fruit of love is flourishing in our hearts as it should, there is no room for prejudice of any kind. The playing field is level in Christ. God's love frees us to truly accept others as our brothers and sisters in Christ—our equal, regardless of gender, race, nationality, denominational affiliation, or even Bible school association. We should be free to worship with all believers and not be threatened or bothered by our differences.

Why, then, is there so much division and strife within our churches and between the churches themselves? Why is there still prejudice within the Church? The answer is plain and simple—because we have not died to self! It should not surprise us that there is so much disunity within the Body of Christ when self is allowed to rule.

The good news is we have the power to change this. Each of us must get to the place where we can say, "It's not about me. It's all about Jesus. I died! I am a 'dead man (or woman) walking' because my life is now hidden in Christ Jesus. It's no longer I who live but Christ lives in me. He is love, and He loves through me." The only one getting the glory in our divisions and strife is the devil! Let us determine not to give him any place.

A Word Specifically about Racial Prejudice

I am aware of the potential hazard in attempting to tackle racial prejudice, which exists not only in the United States but all over the world. This is especially true since I am a member of an offending race (Caucasian), but I believe there is much that needs to be said about this to the Church. I do not pretend to have all the answers to this complex issue, but I believe the Lord has given me some insight that I would like to share.

Under the Pickle?

When pride and ignorance are mixed together, the result is a volatile opportunity for prejudice. The majority race will take advantage of and dominate those of the minority. This has been the white man's sin in the United States. But the issue is not one sided. When bitterness and offense are combined with pride, an equally volatile equation results, such as has plagued the Native American and African American communities. But this problem is not relegated to the United States. The Aborigines of Australia and many other people groups around the world have suffered similarly.

Understand that I am not in any way condemning those who have been the victims of prejudice. It is easy to understand their bitterness and resentment. In fact, I find it hard to blame them for it. As true followers of Jesus Christ, however, we must rise above this. Prejudice in unbelievers is one thing; but as Christians, we are held to a much higher standard—whether we are the offenders or the ones who have been offended. We are commanded to live by the royal law of love.

The bottom line, as I have observed it, is that when people place too much emphasis on their race, nationality, or any factor other than Christ, they have not settled the identity issue. If you have not already done so, determine to view all people as created by God. Remember that He loves us all the same and plays no favorites. He is the author of all nations, cultures, and races. He loves variety, so we should too. Let us celebrate our differences and use them to strengthen one another rather than allowing them to divide us.

The Heavenly Vision for the Church

The apostle Peter overcame his prejudices in an amazing way. One morning while he was ministering to the Lord in Joppa at Simon the Tanner's house, he had a vision from the Lord. In the vision, he saw all kinds of nonkosher animals, ones that the Jews were forbidden by Levitical law to eat. A voice said, "Get up, Peter. Kill and eat" (Acts 10:13). To this Peter responded emphatically that he had never eaten such food and that he was not about to start, thank you very much!

The voice spoke again, "Do not call anything impure that God has made clean" (v. 15). This was repeated three times, no doubt, for emphasis. Peter got the message and immediately acted upon it. The next day he went to the Gentile Cornelius' house to share the Good News, and thus began the movement of the Church to take the Gospel to *all* people, not only the Jews.

The message from this vision is quite simple. Do not call any group of people unworthy or unfit for the Gospel, because God has created all peoples in His image and declared every one of them worthy to receive His love. To reject or insult anyone is to reject or insult God himself. No race is excluded.

Evidently Barnabas and Peter worked through this issue, and we would do well to follow their example. When a person's identity is truly in Christ, accepting others is easy. After all, since God loves all people, when you are full of His love, it is easy for you love people of all colors and to appreciate the cultural and racial diversity with which God has blessed us. I believe this is heaven's vision for the Church—to be full of people from every race, tribe, and tongue. He even said so!

> I looked and there before me was a great multitude that no one could count, from every nation, tribe, people and language, standing before the throne and in front of the Lamb. They were wearing white robes and were holding palm branches in their hands.
>
> Revelation 7:9

Secure believers set a righteous example by accepting all people, regardless of background, race, or any other thing. The result? "The fruit of the righteous is a tree of life" (Prov. 11:30). Concerning them, no one ever asks, "Where's the fruit?"

Lord, I am growing as a result of my vertical relationship with You, and I ask You to help me keep our communication free flowing. Help me never to put You in a box or grow stagnant or legalistic but to remain open to Your Spirit, especially when You do a new thing. Help me to see all people as You see them, to love and accept them as You do. Cause fruit to abound in me so that everyone I come into contact with may partake of the bounty. Amen.

CHAPTER 7

Risk Takers

IT HAS BEEN MY EXPERIENCE that every believer falls into one of two groups: *risk* takers or *care* takers. The risk takers are those who are willing to risk everything in order to obey God and fulfill His call upon their lives. Care takers, on the other hand, are the believers who are content with taking care of what they have. They are comfortable and secure and rarely, if ever, take the risk of stepping out in faith and believing God for growth and expansion in their lives.

Which one are you?

Jesus dealt with this issue in the parable commonly known as the Parable of the Talents, which is basically a story about risk, using money as the example. In the story, a nobleman was going on a long trip and gave his servants some money with instructions to put the money to work. Upon his return, he followed up on his servants. Two had invested the money resulting in increase. A third servant had hidden the money out of fear, much to the dismay of his master because it had not yielded any growth at all. *The Message* version of the Bible fittingly states the "moral of the story":

> "Risk your life and get more than you ever dreamed of. Play it safe and end up holding the bag."
>
> Luke 19:26

Why is it that some people are willing to take risks and others are not? Why can some people jump out in faith and seemingly take huge steps while others just vacillate and never seem to go anywhere? No doubt, there are many answers to these questions, but I believe that our identity in Christ plays a large role.

This brings up two of the significant fruits on the tree in our analogy: trust and rock-solid faith. In order for believers to willingly take risks, these two elements must be present.

Our Personal Story

On June 1, 1996, Lisa and I took one of those gigantic steps of faith. Up to that time Lisa had been an elementary

school teacher in a local public school system, and I had been on the pastoral staff of Victory Christian Center in Tulsa, Oklahoma. Then the Lord led us to resign our positions and launch into our own ministry.

This was all well and good except for one minor detail—we had no idea how we would survive financially. At the time we had bills and even some debt. We did not have a single committed supporter and not one pastor had invited us to minister in his church.

In our minds, this was huge! Had we heard from God? Were we really ready to leave the comforts of solid employment and transition to live by faith (receive our support solely from other believers)? I remember it seemed as if earthquakes and volcanoes were erupting in my stomach. My mind screamed, *This is not a good time for us to do this! What if you fall flat on your face? You have a reputation of being a solid guy. Why go and throw that away?*

But ... we had a promise from God! We knew we had heard from Him and that it was His will for us to take this step. He reassured our hearts that we would not be diminished, and we have not been.

Arriving at the place in our walk with God where we could obey Him in such weighty matters did not happen overnight. This was the result of a lifelong process of learning to hear His voice and obeying Him in the everyday little things. He had guided us, and we had also witnessed His faithfulness to provide. We firmly believed that what He had done for us in the past, He would do again. We did not know *how* He would do it, but we trusted that He would take care of everything concerning us. And, He has! We have never been late on a payment because of a lack of funds. We have been able to travel around the globe and minister in more than thirty nations. And God has paid for it all!

We could have easily justified staying in our respective jobs and "played it safe." We had nice positions and a measure of security. In fact, the reasons to stay far outweighed the ones to launch out! But we knew we would be outside the will of God if we did not step out and follow our hearts. Had we chosen to stay where we were, I am certain that we would have forever wondered what would have happened had we obeyed God when He directed us.

In retrospect, one of the greatest things I had going for me was an identity rooted in Christ and the personal security that flows from it. The *Barnabas Factor* made all the difference in the world. Without it, I do not think I could have launched out and fully obeyed the Lord.

East Bank

Many believers who are too insecure never really reach their destiny—God's dream for their lives. They sit, if you will, on the eastern bank of the Jordan River, at flood stage, and longingly look over into the Promised Land on the

western side. The Promised Land is a land that flows with milk and honey. It is the place where your needs are met and God's dream for your life is realized. It represents a place of victory.

"But, God, I am afraid of failure! I am afraid because the river is swollen. I might be swept away in its strong current!"

Because of their fears, many have never obeyed and taken that first step of faith. Consequently they have never seen the miracles that God would have performed to ensure their safe crossing. When Joshua and the priests took the first step, the Jordan River parted, but they had to take that first step in faith before they saw the miracles!

I am sure that Joshua's mind was screaming at him as mine screamed at me. He was the leader of over one million former slaves, only a handful of whom probably knew how to swim. Think of their livestock! How could he get them all safely across the Jordan River at flood stage? It would take a miracle, and that is just what they had. But it was the result of that first a step of faith.

The majority of people are waiting for the miracles to start before they launch out into the deep, but that is not the way God usually works. He likes faith. He is waiting for us to take Him at His Word, to take that first step; but when we do, He will never let us down. The miracles will be there when we need them.

Trust

It all boils down to trust. It takes a real security in Christ to transfer the control of our lives over to Him, but that is what being a risk taker is all about. Risk takers realize that they do not belong to themselves but to Christ. Their identity is found in Him. They are not motivated by self-preservation or self-promotion. Their only aim is to please God. They are not driven by fear, but they are led by the Holy Spirit and their love for God.

So what about you? Are you a risk taker, willing to obey God at any cost? Or, are you a care taker, tending to hold back, choosing to take care of things the way they are rather than follow God's leading? If the latter describes you, insecurity may be at the root. Take the matter to the Father and explore your heart together. There is nothing to be afraid of. All of His plans are good and by following His leading, your life will better than you have ever dreamed.

Barnabas' Sandals

I consider risk taking to be a fruit of the *Barnabas Factor* at work in a person's life. The reason I say this is because Barnabas was willing to take risks that most people would shy away from. This will be apparent as we continue to read about him.

> When [Saul] came to Jerusalem, he tried to join the disciples, but they were all afraid of him, not believing that he really was a disciple. But Barnabas took him and brought him to the apostles. He told them how Saul on his journey had seen the Lord and that the Lord had spoken to him, and how in Damascus he had preached fearlessly in the name of Jesus. So Saul stayed with them and moved about freely in Jerusalem, speaking boldly in the name of the Lord.
>
> Acts 9:26–28

If you put yourself in Barnabas' sandals, you can understand that he was taking a huge risk by meeting with Paul and introducing him to the apostles. Evidently the word among the believers in Jerusalem had been that Paul's visit was just a plot by the Jews to infiltrate the Church. Since Paul had spent most of the three years following his conversion in the Arabian Desert, only the believers in Damascus knew for sure that his conversion experience was genuine. It was natural for those who did not know him to be skeptical of this man who had been one of the most zealous persecutors of the Church.

What enabled Barnabas to take this risk with Paul? After all, Barnabas was well respected. It is amazing to realize that instead of trying to protect his own image, Barnabas was willing to put his reputation on the line for a man he did not even know. We can only surmise that he had either received a revelation from the Holy Spirit about Paul or he was operating in his gift as an encourager, choosing to believe the best. More than likely it was a little of both. How different

Church history might be had Barnabas not taken this risk and gone to meet Paul and connected him with the apostles!

One of the greatest fruits of a life rooted in Christ's identity is a willingness to obey God no matter how difficult or dangerous it may seem at the moment. The secret is a deep-seated trust in Him. This trust that cannot be easily explained to those who have never experienced it, but it enables these believers to take risks and steps of faith that others do not readily take. Because of that, the risk takers are advancing the Kingdom while the insecure care takers are sitting at home wondering what it would have been like if they had only obeyed God.

What about you? At the end of your days are you going to be more disappointed about the risks you took and failed or the fact that you never took the risks in the first place? Are you going to be thankful for the great blessings and miracles that came as a result of your risk taking, or will you be content that you shrunk back from God's perfect will for your life and settled for the status quo, merely taking care of your personal world?

A Great Risk Taker

Often being a risk taker requires stepping out in the face of family members who disagree or do not understand the step of faith. Such was the case for one of two brothers in

Risk Takers

nineteenth-century England. The older of these brothers chose to become a surgeon. He did well in his profession, becoming famous and quite wealthy. The younger brother, however, felt the call to become a missionary to Africa. This was during a time when twenty-three out of twenty-five missionaries did not live longer than two years after arriving on the continent. Most even left home with all their possessions in a pine coffin because they knew they would probably come back in it! Now, that's commitment! Evidentally they felt that taking the Gospel to those who had never heard it was a cause worth being passionate about!

Because of these inherent risks, the surgeon tried to dissuade his younger sibling from going to Africa. He said, "You will never come back alive, and you will die in obscurity. You are wasting your life!"

Today, the older brother has about two sentences dedicated to him in the *Encyclopedia Britannica.* But his words are found within the several pages dedicated to the younger brother, David Livingstone, who is credited with opening the interior of Africa to Jesus. When this great missionary died after years of faithful service, the Africans cut his heart out and buried it in Africa, because they said that even though Livingstone was outwardly a white man, his heart was African.

David Livingstone's body is buried at Westminster Abbey in London where the heroes of the British Empire are buried. So much for dying in obscurity! This fearless believer pursued his passion and the call of God, even in the face of intense opposition, and God honored him.

Today, 150 years later, the Church is expanding rapidly throughout sub-Sahara Africa and great credit is due to the courageous risk takers of the nineteenth century who sacrificially laid down their lives for the sake of the Gospel. They established the foundation from which we in this generation are reaping a massive harvest. We are the fortunate ones to live during this generation, but I believe that they are the truly blessed ones who will receive the greater reward in heaven for their faithfulness.

David Livingstone once wrote: "Future missionaries will be rewarded by conversions for every sermon. ... Let them not forget ... us, who worked when all was gloom, and no evidence of success in the way of conversions cheered our paths."

What about You?

Perhaps you want to start a new business, go back to school, witness to your neighbor, begin tithing, buy a new house, or even begin a new ministry; but you feel like a deer in the headlights of an eighteen-wheeler when you think about it. If this is what God is leading you to do, then take that step in faith and do it! Trust God to faithfully lead you across your Jordan and into the Promised Land. It is natural to feel apprehension whenever you begin something new, but if you have a sure foundation in Christ, it makes it much easier to do.

If you find that you just cannot take that step of faith, then I encourage you to examine the condition of your root system. Is it healthy or diseased? Where is your identity rooted? This could give you a clue as to why it is difficult for you to begin what God is leading you to do.

You Need a Sponsor

We mentioned that Barnabas was willing to risk his reputation on Paul. An additional risk he took was in becoming Paul's *sponsor*. Many young men and women need a sponsor—someone who is experienced in ministry who will validate the newcomer's ministry and life. Because the apostles and the believers in Jerusalem trusted Barnabas, they accepted Paul. Without this endorsement, Paul probably would not have been received so easily.

Risk takers not only take big steps of faith for themselves, but they are also willing to take risks with others. If you notice someone with potential, but you also see that much refinement is needed, it may be God's way of asking you to take a risk on that person, similar to the one Barnabas took with Paul.

When I first began in the ministry, Pastor Bob Pate did this for me. Several years my senior, he saw potential in me and took me under his wing, allowing me to minister in his pulpit and to become the youth pastor of his church. He lovingly critiqued my teachings and mentored me in all aspects of ministry. As a result I progressed rapidly in my ministry gifts. Pastor Bob also introduced me to many people in the ministry where we lived. To this day some of those churches are among our biggest supporters. I seriously doubt I would be where I am today had it not been for this generous man, and I am eternally grateful for the risks he was willing to take on me.

Mentors Needed

Sad to say, veteran ministers like Pastor Bob are rare. Because so many are insecure or consumed with themselves, they are not willing to reach out unselfishly to help the young Pauls get started. What a wonderful gift it would be to these burgeoning ministers to have a Barnabas come alongside and say, "Allow me to introduce you to the others." I believe there are many great Pauls who slip through the cracks of the Church because there are not enough secure men and women to mentor and sponsor them.

Being a mentor is not a high-profile ministry that yields a great deal of affirmation. It is more of a behind-the-scenes type of work that requires a secure individual. A true sponsor is an outwardly focused person who genuinely loves people and is actively on the alert, looking for "diamonds in the rough." Like the prophet Samuel recognized the gift in David, a godly sponsor will spot these upstarts who may not even register on the radar screen of most people.

Risk Takers

In this generation, many emerging leaders may not look like the ones of the past. Many of our present-day Pauls may have tattoos, body-piercing, and even purple hair! When you see this type of individual, you might think, *Good Lord, help us all!* But the Holy Spirit may say, *That young lady needs your help. I want you to mentor her for ministry because I have called her to a great work.*

Mentors and sponsors are not only needed in the ministry, but they are needed throughout the Body of Christ. One area of great importance is in the lives of young men and women who are being raised in single-parent homes. While the existing parent may be doing a fine job, a godly mentor may be just what the young person needs to fill in some of the gaps left by the missing parent. Boys desperately need the input of secure male believers, so they can become strong godly men. Young girls need godly, secure women to teach them how to be ladies. Being a sponsor to one of these young people can make an eternal difference in their lives and result in a deeply satisfying experience for the mentor.

People Lovers

One of the hallmarks of a Christian should be that we sincerely love all people. It is by this fruit of love that we can measure how properly we are rooted in the Lord. If things are as they should be in our walk with Him, a genuine love will rise up in us for *all* people—both the lovely and the unlovely, regardless of any idiosyncrasies they might possess.

Human nature, on the other hand, tries to avoid those who are different or just plain weird. When I find myself pulling back from people whom I am not comfortable with, I have to remind myself that Jesus did not come for the well, normal, beautiful, "got it together" people. He came for the sick, the unlovely, the needy, the misfits—those who are far from perfect.

A situation came up early in my ministry that taught me this lesson in a powerful way. At the conclusion of a particular service, several other leaders and I were praying with members of the church who had come forward. I noticed that one of the men coming toward us was a little different. As soon as he began speaking, I could tell that he was one of those people who could talk incessantly without ever saying anything of substance. I hate to admit it, but I saw him as a time robber. Many times while listening to him drone on, I thought to myself, *I have been listening to him for several minutes, and I have no idea what he just said.* Because of a previous lifestyle involving heavy drug usage, he had trouble connecting his thoughts.

After a while I noticed that the other leaders who had been praying with me had disappeared. To say the least, I was perturbed. I was the only one left to pray with this man, or should I say listen to him.

At that instant, the Holy Spirit impressed on me that Jesus would not have left. He would have stayed and prayed with this man and that I should always do the same. This experience gave me a greater understanding of the real purpose of ministry—reaching *all* people, not just the ones I feel comfortable with. God knew I would need this in the years to come.

Seeing Them as They Will Become

Many times while ministering around the world, sometimes in shanty towns, I encounter people who are filthy, have matted hair, are wearing tattered clothing, and smell rather rank. My natural inclination is to recoil, but I have learned to look past outward appearances and see these people as God does. They are created in the image of God and are just as deserving of experiencing His love as I am. That is when true compassion flows through us to change people. (See Mark 1:40–45.)

Most of us are not naturally mercy oriented, so I believe it takes a secure person in Christ to learn how to be. We must put on the eyes of compassion in order to see past where people are right now and envision them as they will become.

King David's family only saw him as an insignificant shepherd boy when he was young, but God saw him differently. He saw a king! (See 1 Samuel 16:1–13.) We, too, must see the

THE *B*ARNABAS FACTOR

potential in people. Barnabas did. That is why he took the risk to introduce Paul to the leaders of the Jerusalem church. As we will later see, Paul (knowing firsthand the impact of such a blessing) took a similar risk with another major player in the early Church—Timothy, to whom Paul wrote the New Testament letters bearing the young protégé's name.

About seeing the best in people and being willing to take risks on them, I want to share one more thought with you. Unfortunately there may be times when you try to reach out to someone, but you are not received and your help is not welcome. It takes wisdom to know when you have done all you can and it is time to move on. An insecure believer would likely take this as rejection and refuse to keep looking for the next Paul. But do not let this be said of you! Keep looking for those who have a genuine teachable spirit and pour into their lives.

In summary, faith-filled risk takers lead exciting lives that exceed their dreams. Like Barnabas they bear abundant fruit and live their lives with no regrets. They simply pray, hear, and obey. May we go and do likewise.

> *Father, I ask you to produce more secure leaders like Barnabas for the young Pauls in the Body of Christ. We need them in this final hour to train the laborers for the incredible harvest coming in all over the world! In the areas where I need to be mentored, I ask you to bring a Barnabas into my life. Then help me to be secure enough to recognize the Pauls in my midst and use me to mentor them. Give me the courage to be a risk taker for You. Amen.*

CHAPTER 8

What Does God Say?

WHEN OTHERS DESCRIBE YOU, what words do they use? Are their descriptions merely physical in nature, or do they refer to your intangible qualities like integrity, a heart for God, dependability, or intelligence? Do you have a good reputation among those who know you?

Proverbs offers an important reminder:

A good name is more desirable than great riches; to be esteemed is better than silver or gold.

Proverbs 22:1

Not enough can be said of the value of a good name. It can take years to earn one, and a great deal of wisdom is required to maintain it. The investment is well worth the effort, however. Unfortunately a good name can be lost in only a moment, so one should take great pains to protect it.

If you think about it, young people have to prove their trustworthiness and dependability much more so than older adults. Older people are usually given the benefit of the doubt. Given their age and years of experience, it is assumed that they have some wisdom, unless they have done something to jeopardize that reputation. On the other hand, most have very little expectation for youth. Because of their limited life experience, most assume they do not know much.

These assumptions are not always correct! Paul, now a seasoned minister, was mindful of this tendency and exhorted his young protégé, Timothy:

> Don't let anyone look down on you because you are young, but set an example for the believers in speech, in life, in love, in faith and in purity.
>
> 1 Timothy 4:12

> Flee the evil desires of youth, and pursue righteousness, faith, love and peace, along with those who call on the Lord out of a pure heart.
>
> 2 Timothy 2:22

David shared an important key along this line in the Old Testament:

What Does God Say?

> How can a young man keep his way pure?
> By living according to your word.
>
> Psalm 119:9

For believers, reputation is paramount because our lives are supposed to be a reflection of Christ. What the non-Christians believe concerning Christ by and large comes from the Christ that believers have presented to them through words and actions—good or bad. Sadly, much has been done in the name of Christ through the ages that He has had absolutely nothing to do with. Charles Finney, the great nineteenth-century revivalist and abolitionist, once stated: "Christians are the single greatest reason others come to Christ, but they are also the single greatest reason others reject Christ." There is a direct correlation between our actions and how unbelievers respond to our message.

Even more important that our reputation among people, however, is what *God* thinks of us. How would He describe you? What qualities stand out to Him? The writer of Acts gives us a rare glimpse into the Holy Spirit's description of a person. About Barnabas, He inspired the writer to pen these words:

> He was a good man, full of the Holy Spirit and faith, and a great number of people were brought to the Lord.
>
> Acts 11:24

Notice the qualities that stood out to Him, the characteristics that the Holy Spirit considered important enough to mention:

- a good man
- full of the Holy Spirit
- full of faith

Could the same be said of you? It will do us good to examine each of these aspects of the *Barnabas Factor* in depth.

A Good Man

This description reveals two things. First, it speaks of character. As we discussed in an earlier chapter, integrity grows from a healthy identity in Christ. I will not say much more concerning it but to note that this was the first trait to be highlighted. Contrary to what contemporary society believes, character and integrity do matter, especially to the Lord; consequently, they should matter to us.

Can people trust you? Is your word good? When you say something, do people believe you; or do they wonder whether or not you are telling the truth? How others answer these questions about you has a tremendous impact on the way in which they respond to you. I have often heard people when looking for a car repairman, for example, say something like, "I know he is little more expensive than the others, but he is honest." To most people integrity is more valuable than finding the best price.

Second, the fact that Barnabas was considered "a good man" tells us a great deal about him. I believe it indicates

that he possessed a genuine love for people and that he treated them with dignity and respect, giving every individual his full attention. He must have been good and fair to everyone, regardless of a person's position, status, race, or any other factor. I doubt that it mattered whether or not people were his employees, his financial supporters, or even if they liked him, although how could anyone *not* have liked such a terrific individual? I imagine Barnabas was also lavish with genuine praise and expressed his appreciation to others freely. Had he not been all of these things, I doubt that the Holy Spirit would have inspired the writer to describe him as a "good man." The fact was, Barnabas was a truly good man in every sense of the word.

A Lesson from Dad

I have firsthand experience with a man like this—my dad. He taught me the invaluable lesson that we should treat everyone we meet with dignity, respect, and appreciation. When I was in college, I worked several summers on the maintenance crew at the corporate headquarters where my dad was an executive. There were other sons of executives who were summer workers as well, but my dad was the only executive that the maintenance men knew. The reason was that he always made it a point to speak to them and to ask how they were doing. He would give them a firm handshake and look them in the eye when he spoke to them. Because of his friendliness and genuine concern for them, they all liked him. These kind actions did not take him any more than ten to fifteen seconds of his "busy" time, but it meant the world to these laborers. They told me so.

I even had people ask me on the elevator, "Are you Harold Boehm's son?"

"Yes, sir," I would respond.

They would invariably proceed to tell me how nice of a man my father was. You know what else stood out to them? They all knew that he was a committed Christian. I am confident that the Jesus he projected made a positive impression on them.

Significant Others

How do you treat the people who, based upon their jobs, are often considered insignificant—the parking lot attendant, the cashier at the grocery store, the waitress, the garbage man, the person behind the airline ticket counter, or the bank teller? Given that most people treat these folks as though they were invisible, imagine the positive impact you can have by always making a point to give them your attention and affirmation. In our own lives, Lisa and I always leave a nice tip at restaurants, and if the waitperson does a good job, we tell him or her. It is amazing how they light up when we compliment them. You know what is important

about that? They also see us bow our heads to pray over our food. It is important the kind of Jesus we project to them.

How do you treat your co-workers or those who work for you? Do they know that you appreciate them? Or, is the only time they hear from you when they make a mistake? Do you let them know the ways they bless you and the organization? Or, do you have the attitude that your employees should feel blessed that they even have a job?

Regardless of the roles people fill in life, they are just that—people! And all people need relationships. Almost everyone responds positively to those who reach out on a relational level. Take ten seconds of your time and tell the people in your world that you appreciate them. Commending a whole group is good, but singling people out and telling them on an individual basis has the greatest impact.

If you will do this regularly, these people will climb the highest mountain and cross the widest sea for you! Why? Because you have made invaluable deposits into their lives and made them feel significant. If you have to always remind your workers to be there at the right time and to work hard, it is probably a good indication that their relational accounts are low. What can you do today to make some deposits?

It's All in the Details

Remembering people's names is a way to make a great relational deposit. Recalling details about their lives is a powerful investment as well. I often hear people say that they are not very good at remembering details or names, but the truth is, people remember what they want to remember. What do you think it says to others when someone remembers their name? It says, "You are valuable and important!"

In my own life, when I learn specific details about people, I incorporate those things into the subsequent conversations I have with them. These individuals are often surprised that I remember what they have shared with me, but it is my way of letting them know they are significant and important to me. I believe Jesus was this kind of man. Why? Because people are important to God. He created every person on the planet in His image and each of us is equally significant to Him. Secure men and women like Barnabas are good people who understand this and willingly take the time to touch people's lives on a relational level. They want to connect to others and to demonstrate the same love that the Father has shown them. Even though we did not deserve it and were even enemies of God, He reached out to us with His Son Jesus Christ. Should we not find it within ourselves to show that same love to others?

Bring It Home

Let us bring this discussion home—literally. How do you treat your spouse and children? Some people are good at showing love to others, but they do not know how to

demonstrate that same love and appreciation to their own family. Often men are not as verbal as their wives. It is common to hear men say, "My family should know how much I appreciate them. After all, I provide for them, don't I?" While wives and children may appreciate financial provision and material possessions, the thing they need most is a relationship with the most important man in their lives. If your family has not been responding to you the way you feel they should, perhaps it is a good time to give yourself a checkup. Time, verbal expressions of love and appreciation, and meaningful conversation are key elements necessary for a happy family.

Husbands, have you verbally told your wife that you appreciate her? Do you praise her in front of others where she can hear it? She, as well as your children, needs to hear these things on a regular basis.

Wives, does your husband know how much you appreciate him and his hard work? Instead of complaining about the things he has or has not done, begin giving him genuine compliments for the positive aspects of his life. You may be amazed at the transformation that will take place. Nearly every successful man I have ever met has a supportive wife. You play a huge role in his success, and he needs to hear positive words of affirmation from you.

If you will remember, Barnabas was a great encourager to the believers at Antioch. (See Acts 11:23.) When the Holy Spirit referred to him as a "good man," no doubt this is one reason why. From this quality alone, it is easy to understand why the revival at Antioch grew under Barnabas' leadership. It is amazing what a few genuine words of encouragement and appreciation can do in the lives of people.

Full of the Holy Spirit

The second characteristic the Holy Spirit used to describe Barnabas was that he was "full of the Holy Spirit." When I think of Christians fitting this description, I envision men and women who are full of life, enthusiasm, and victory. Their zest is contagious. We have said it before, but it bears repeating: the key to this kind of life is being connected to the Source through daily times of fellowship with Him—daily "fill ups," if you will. There really is no other way to maintain this level of enthusiasm on a consistent basis. But it is this lifestyle that draws unbelievers to Christ and nominal Christians to a deeper walk with God.

I find it interesting that the word *enthusiasm* is derived from the Greek language and literally means "in God."[3] If we are in God and He is in us, then life and enthusiasm will flow from us to those whose lives we touch! Our level of enthusiasm is a good indicator as to how filled with the Spirit we are. If your enthusiasm is lagging, pull off the road for a bit and reconnect to the Source. When you have drunk your fill, then head back out to be a blessing.

An encounter with someone like Barnabas always leaves a person feeling better than before. Are you that type of person? When people see you, do they usually see a warm smile on your face? Are you approachable and easy to talk to? Do you deflect the attention from yourself to the needs of the person you are with?

These are earmarks of the Spirit-filled life we are meant to live. It comes from having our security in Christ with our focus on Him and others, rather than on ourselves or our inadequacies. It is all about serving people because that is the true Spirit of Jesus living inside us.

Gifts or Fruit?

People full of the Holy Spirit also have His gifts present in their lives. They know God's voice well and are faithful to follow His leading. Some have tried to de-emphasize the gifts of the Spirit and only focus on the fruit of the Spirit, as though this were an indication of a more serious walk with God. It may sounds noble, but it is unbiblical according to the apostle Paul! He said,

> Follow the way of love *and* eagerly desire spiritual gifts, especially the gift of prophecy.
>
> 1 Corinthians 14:1 (emphasis added)

After meditating on this verse one day, it came to me that we are not to diminish the importance of the gifts *or* the fruit of the Spirit. After all, they both come from the same Holy Spirit, and they are both vital to the life of the Church and the building up of believers. It is clear to me that He wants us to pursue both. So now I strive to bear the fruit of love, for example, but I also desire the Holy Spirit's gifts at the same time. I believe that Barnabas was a man who exhibited both.

Full of Faith

The third characteristic that the Holy Spirit highlighted in describing Barnabas was that he was "full of faith." We can see how strongly He feels about this quality by reading Hebrews 11:6, which states: "Without faith it is impossible to please God." Since Barnabas was full of faith, he obviously pleased His Father, and as we detailed in a previous chapter, faith is a fruit of secure believers.

Faith-filled believers are positive people, possibility thinkers. The word *impossible* is not even in their vocabulary. Why do they have such confidence? Because they know that all things are possible with God. (Matt. 17:20–21; Luke 1:37.) These individuals rarely complain or speak in negative terms. Doubt and fear are foreign to them. They are confident that God is working all things out for their good, regardless of what the circumstances look like. Faith-filled believers think "outside of the box" and do not put any limitations on God and what He wants to do through them.

They know they serve a big God who dreams big dreams! (See Eph. 3:20.)

Giant-sized Faith

When I think of someone who was full of faith, I immediately think of David, the shepherd boy who challenged the giant Goliath. Even though Goliath was over nine feet tall and was an experienced warrior, David did not flinch in his presence or in the face of his intimidating taunts. David—armed with only his sling shot and five smooth stones from a nearby stream—said to Goliath, "You come against me with sword and spear and javelin, but I come against you in the name of the LORD Almighty. ... This day the LORD will hand you over to me" (1 Sam. 17:45–46). And we know the outcome—David prevailed. No earthly giant was any match for his giant God. What an example of faith!

For faith-filled believers, it does not matter what the circumstances look like. They take God at His Word and act on it.

Another Giant in Faith

William Carey, an Englishman considered to be the father of the modern missions movement, was another faith-filled believer. His personal motto was, "Expect great things from God! Attempt great things for God!" This came from a man who faced tremendous obstacles such as sickness, the death of family members, poverty, unjust criticism, and a horrible fire, to name a few. Yet through his faith in God, William Carey persevered. Born in 1761 to humble beginnings, this man became a cobbler by trade and possessed nothing more than a junior-high-level education. In the midst of mending the shoes of others, however, he caught God's passion to fulfill the Great Commission.

Attempting to share his newfound passion with a group of pastors, Carey was sharply rebuked and then forbidden to speak on the subject again. Not to be deterred, he then channeled his enthusiasm into writing a book on the Church's mandate to complete the Great Commission. This little book sparked a vast movement in both England and the United States of young men and women answering the call to go to the nations with the Gospel!

Carey himself left England in 1792, and headed to India, where he eventually died in 1834. But despite meager financial backing, he literally changed the world. By the end of his life, Carey had translated the entire Bible into 6 Indian languages and the New Testament and Gospels into 29 other languages! He had taught himself Latin, Greek, Hebrew, Dutch, French, and several Indian languages. Furthermore, he and his co-laborers started over one hundred Christian schools, which eventually trained more than eight thousand children. The first Christian college in

Asia, which he opened, is still in existence today; and many in India credit him for paving the way for their country's independence. *Impossible* was not in William Carey's vocabulary because he knew he served a big God. His seemingly endless number of accomplishments attest to the fact that he practiced what he preached, tirelessly attempting great things for God while expecting great things from Him—and God never let him down.

Believers who are full of faith like Barnabas, King David, and William Carey are fruitful! Faith and fruitfulness go hand in hand.

The Net Result

Combine goodness with being full of the Holy Spirit and faith and the result is a dynamic believer who bears great fruit for the Kingdom of God! Because Barnabas exhibited these three qualities, the Antiochian revival flourished under his leadership and "a great number of people were brought to the Lord" Acts 11:24.

This is a perfect example of the correlation between the believer's life and the receptivity of others to the message. Fruit draws people! When the world sees believers who are secure in themselves and their position in Christ, who are genuinely good people of integrity, and who are full of the Holy Spirit and faith, great numbers will be brought to the

Lord just as they were in Barnabas' day! That should be sufficient motivation for all of us to develop these same qualities in our own lives.

> *Lord, we desperately need more "good" men and women who are "full of the Holy Spirit and faith" in our churches today. Help me, as well as all believers, to grow up in these areas so that You can use us to the utmost in the next great revival. Amen.*

CHAPTER 9

Mayday! Mayday!

"MAYDAY! MAYDAY!" You may have heard this shouted in war movies, when a pilot has been shot out of the sky. It is a distress signal indicating that the pilot needs immediate assistance. When I was a little boy, I used to love to watch the old WWII movies with my dad. Back then they were not as violent as they are today.

What has always impressed me about the military is how they work so well together and how they are so quick to reinforce one another. When one unit or individual sends out a distress signal, another group is not far behind to bring the needed assistance. In fact, the U.S. Marines have a policy of never leaving any of their wounded behind. They know how to work together, and they never go it alone!

Although the revival at Antioch had not reached the point where Barnabas was sending out distress signals, we do know that "a great number of people" had been added to the church under his leadership. Because the *Barnabas Factor* was at work in his life, he was able to swallow his pride and do something not often seen among Christian leaders. Much of what I am going to say in this chapter will be put in the context of leadership, but it is certainly applicable to everyday life as well. We pick up the narrative here:

> Then Barnabas went to Tarsus to look for Saul [Paul], and when he found him, he brought him to Antioch. So for a whole year Barnabas and Saul met with the church and taught great numbers of people. The disciples were called Christians first at Antioch.
>
> Acts 11:25–26

Let's put this in a modern-day context, so we can get a clear understanding of what happened. Imagine that Barnabas has become a big celebrity in Christian circles. He is the leader of the largest revival on the planet, and people are flocking to Antioch from far and wide to take part. The apostle Peter has even flown in. (Gal. 2:11.) Barnabas has become a household name among Christians and his fame is spreading. *Charisma* and *Christianity Today* have run cover stories, and he is the most sought-after guest on Christian radio and television. Life-size placards of Barnabas holding his bestselling

new book greet every customer at Christian bookstores. People are eager to hear what he has to say and want to know everything he is doing to make the revival a success.

Going back to our text, on the surface it does not appear that Barnabas did anything remarkable. He simply sought the help of Paul. However, when we consider his highly visible and influential position and when we consider the dynamics and egos that are often present in Christian leadership, what Barnabas did was huge! We learn two things about Barnabas. First we can see that he was wise. With no indication that the growth from the revival would slow down anytime soon, Barnabas was proactive. He sought help before the need became critical.

Second, we see what an incredibly humble man Barnabas was. In the midst of all the notoriety and fame that he no doubt was receiving (relative to that time in history), he came to an extremely important realization. He knew his limitations; he realized that alone, he could only take the revival so far. In order to take the movement to the next level, he knew that he was going to need help. I think he also understood that although God had anointed him in certain ways, he by no means had everything the people needed to grow spiritually. By bringing in Paul, Barnabas could expose the people to additional ministry gifts and Paul's personal strengths. The movement would be much more well rounded.

Think about it. When you stretch out one of your arms, you can only reach so far. The span of your arm has a limit.

But when you join hands with another person, the arm span is doubled, even tripled if the person extends both arms! The same is true in leadership. When leaders combine their gifts—instead of using them to compete against one another—the extent of their ministry is multiplied; they can reach more people. Isn't that what ministry is all about? Barnabas was obviously very secure in his calling, revealing that when the Barnabas Factor *is in operation, a person is* not afraid to ask for help.

Momentum Stoppers

Sadly today, many moves of God have been stunted and lost momentum instead of fulfilling their God-given intention. Leaders and lay people alike scratch their heads and wonder why. While I do not claim to have the last word on the subject, I do believe God has given me some insight from which we can benefit. Like so many, the greatest desire of my heart is to see God have His way in the earth. In order for this to happen, however, we are going to have to deal with these issues head on. Understand that my intention is not to judge what others have or have not done; but I believe we can learn from the mistakes that have been made, make the necessary adjustments, and be better prepared for the next revival.

Mayday! Mayday!

Blinded by the Light

Many leaders today enjoy the spotlight, but it can be blinding. Recognizing the pitfalls can help us to avoid them. A few of them include:

- Not wanting to share the spotlight. Unfortunately, I have witnessed firsthand ministries and churches not wanting to work with others because they might have to share the credit if they did. It is apparent by their actions that if their name is not plastered all over the work, they do not want to be a part of it, regardless of how much glory it would bring to the Lord. Selfishness is at the root of this attitude. Barnabas, on the other hand, yielded to the fruit of love. For the good of the people, he was more than willing to share the ministry with Paul.

- Taking ownership. A leader may begin thinking in terms of *my* revival or *my* church, but selfishness at the root of this attitude as well. Barnabas was more interested in building the Kingdom of God than in building his own ministry empire.

- Glorifying self rather than God. The leader who falls into this trap will eventually forfeit the authority to lead. The reason is that when a leader does this, he or she ceases to operate under God's authority and begins operating under his or her own. This is an extremely unstable place for a Christian leader to stand, and it has preceded the fall of many.

Insecure Leaders

We have spent a great deal of time talking about the importance of finding our security in Christ. Here we will look at some specific issues that can develop in the lives of spiritual leaders when insecurities are not dealt with. They not only bear negative fruit in the leaders' lives, they become momentum stoppers during times of revival.

Self-promotion. I have observed that insecure leaders are often shamefully good at self-promotion. Secure leaders, on the other hand, allow their accomplishments to speak for themselves. They realize that their achievements are for the glory of the Lord anyway.

Several times in my life, I have been in situations where leaders met regularly. I have been amazed at how quickly many begin telling how great they were. I have surmised that when insecure leaders are in the midst of other leaders, they feel compelled to promote themselves, but God clearly forbids this: "Let someone else praise you, not your own mouth" (Proverbs 27:2 NLT).

Paul confronted this issue with the Corinthians:

None of you can get by with blowing your own horn before God. Everything that we have ... comes from God by way

of Jesus Christ. That's why we have the saying, "If you're going to blow a horn, blow a trumpet for God."

1 Corinthians 1:29–31 MSG

When we began Catchfire! Ministries, the Lord showed me that I did not need the responsibility of promoting myself, that *He* would be my public relation's officer. If I would go where He sent me and do what He asked me to do, He would open the doors. He spoke these words to my heart: *If you will build My house, I will build yours,* and He has been faithful to that promise.

Insecure leaders aren't the only self-promoters. Have you noticed how eager some people are to tell you all about themselves? Even if these individuals ask how you are doing, they quickly change the subject back to their own lives? Selfishness is again at the root.

Compromising the Truth. Often in the attempt to look better, insecure leaders slant stories to show themselves in a more favorable light. They may also exaggerate when sharing the numbers of people who have received salvation or miracles through their ministries. For them, the end always justifies the means.

Being performance driven. Insecure leaders are usually performance-oriented rather than obedience-oriented. Because of their deep need to feel significant, they avidly seek the applause and recognition of people, which takes precedence over obeying to the Lord.

Being a people pleaser. Insecure individuals experience much stress in life because there is no way anyone can please everyone all the time. Regardless of how hard a person tries to please or do the right thing, there will always be someone who does not agree or who does not like him or her. I have heard it said that we will serve what we fear. In this case, if we fear man, we will serve man. And if we serve man, we are not serving God.

What does God say about it?

> Fear of man will prove to be a snare, but whoever trusts in the LORD is kept safe.
>
> Proverbs 29:25

God's way is so much better. Those who look to Him for their affirmation experience such freedom and security. Instead of being full of stress and anxiety trying to please people, they are at peace. It is simply a matter of trusting Him.

People pleasing often affects personal appearance. When representing the Lord, I believe we should look our best and conduct ourselves with excellence in every area. However, there are far too many Christians and ministers who are overly concerned about their appearance and their image. A popular television commercial several years ago stated, "Image is everything." But that attitude is worldly and leaves very little room for the Holy Spirit to operate. This is not just a current problem; apparently the early Church dealt with it too according to Peter:

> What matters is not your outer appearance—the styling of your hair, the jewelry you wear, the cut of your clothes—but your inner disposition.
>
> 1 Peter 3:3–4 MSG

Timing. Another inherent danger for insecure leaders is that they have the tendency to promote themselves into positions before they are ready to be there. The mentality is, "If I don't stick up for myself, who else will?" For me, *God* comes to mind. Jesus said, "I have placed before you an open door that no one can shut," (Rev. 3:8), and His timing is always perfect.

One reason why timing is so important in regard to promotion is that our character must be developed to the point that it can handle the new level of responsibility. Many climb the ladder quickly because they have charismatic personalities, but they crack under the weight of the added pressure. In order to become an effective leader, stages in the development of character cannot be skipped. There must be a solid foundation built over time.

This is more than likely the chief reason Joseph, in the Old Testament, had to go through all he did in slavery and in prison before he was elevated to the palace. While Joseph was still a teenager, he received the vision for his life from the Lord. God showed him that he would become a leader of nations and that his brothers would bow down to him.

Joseph's first mistake was that he went out and told everyone about it. Needless to say, his brothers did not receive it very well. At that time in his life, Joseph was just an arrogant kid. He certainly was not ready to lead a nation! Sad to say, sometimes people blame the devil for their hardships when, actually, they have brought the problems upon themselves.

Here is word of wisdom to all who find themselves in Joseph's position: When God reveals a vision for your life, it is wise to keep it to yourself and not share it with others until the timing is right. Remember what Mary, the mother of Jesus, did? After the angel appeared to her and told her about her baby Son, Jesus, the Bible tells us, "Mary treasured up all these things and pondered them in her heart" (Luke 2:19). There is a time to speak, but there is also a time to ponder and pray over what God has revealed.

One of the problems is that most people see you as you are right now. They cannot envision your potential the way that God does. God knows what you will become, but most other people do not. At the time of Joseph's dream, all of his brothers and even his father could only see a regular teenage boy. God, on the other hand, saw a great world leader in the making.

In my own life, in my early twenties, I received insight from the Lord that I would stand before thousands and preach mass crusades around the world. At the time, I was merely a youth pastor with a handful of teens under my direction, and most of them did not want to be there. Because I was the youngest member of the church staff, I often did the menial tasks around the church like opening and closing, sweeping the floors, and cleaning the toilets. I remember walking through the dark church early in the morning turning on lights and unlocking doors and wondering how I was ever going to go from the hills of West Virginia to preach before thousands around the world. Thankfully I had enough wisdom to know that I should keep this to myself and just pray over the thought. At the time, I was not even sure that I believed it myself, much less think anyone else would. It took nearly twenty years before the vision God gave me became a reality, but now I stand before crowds of thousands and proclaim the Good News of Jesus. I have literally seen thousands come to the Lord and watched hundreds receive physical healing!

Why did it take so long? I believe it was because, like Joseph, I was in training. God was forming my character and honing my skills in order that my character and ability would match the responsibility that He would entrust to me. When the door finally opened, I was ready to step through it! Since that time, I have continued to trust God with the timing of all aspects of our ministry, and there is an added bonus: because He is my public relations manager, the items on my itinerary fall into place when they are supposed to. He never double books.

Perhaps God has placed a dream in your heart, but you may be discouraged because so much time has passed. You may be tempted to give up on the dream or to jump out ahead of God and make something happen. I encourage you not to fall into either trap. God knows you better than you know yourself, and you can trust Him to open the necessary doors when all of the conditions are right. His timing really is perfect.

Lack of trust. We have mentioned before that insecure believers have difficulty trusting God, but they also have a hard time trusting people. They make statements like, "You always have to watch your backside. No one else will!" This grieves me because it reveals a lack of trust in the Lord to be one's rearguard. He has promised to be our shield and defender. Barnabas, however, was not plagued with insecurity, so he was able to ask Paul for help without fear of being hurt or burned by the budding minister. Barnabas' main concern was to ensure that the believers at Antioch had what they needed to experience all God had to offer. He trusted God to "watch his backside."

When we take into account all of the negative fruits that insecurity produces in leaders, we see just how remarkable Barnabas' leadership was. Because he was comfortable in his calling, he was able to ask for help when he needed it. Motivated by a desire to obey God and meet the needs of the people, he was not concerned with promoting himself or improving his image to please others. His trust was firmly placed in the Lord. He was a man of integrity who never compromised the truth for his own gain, and he was wise in regard to timing. May the same be said of us.

> *Lord, I pray for those in Christian leadership who are plagued with insecurity as well as for myself. Help us to look to You as our source of security and affirmation. Cause us to desire to please and obey You above all things. Help us to recognize the fruits of insecurity when they manifest, and show us how to replace them with trust in You. Amen.*

CHAPTER 10

Lift the Lid!

SEVERAL YEARS AGO my wife's niece came to stay with us for several months, and she brought Bagira the Cat with her, who was named after the panther in the *Jungle Book*. Because my wife is not fond of animals in the house, the cat was confined to my office in the back of our home. Bagira and I shared quarters for several months. I am not sure she ever accepted me, but she did allow me to rub her tummy from time to time.

We never allowed Bagira to leave the office, but eventually we began leaving the door open and blocking the opening with a baby gate. Although she would longingly look out the door, we were astounded that not once did she ever hop the fence to roam around the rest of the house! She did think about it, however. It was comical to watch her lift her paw like she was going to jump out, but every time she would bring it back, not quite able to bring herself to do it. Amazingly she continued this even after we quit using the gate and left the door wide open! See, in her mind, she could not break out of her preconditioned boundaries to a new level, even though she longed to do so.

We can learn an important lesson from little Bagira. You have heard the phrase "Think outside the box." Well, I like to say, "Lift the lid!" Have you ever found yourself at a certain level in life but it seemed impossible to rise to new heights, like your head kept hitting a lid? Perhaps that describes you today. If so, I have good news—a lid can be opened! Actually, the Lord has already taken the lid *off* and removed all the barriers to our success. Unfortunately, insecurities often keep us confined to the old way of life, much like that gate convinced Bagira that she could not jump over.

While we may be experiencing many blessings in our lives, there may still be issues that hinder us in certain areas. In this chapter, we will discuss some of the qualities that a leader can assimilate—components of the *Barnabas Factor*—that will "lift the lid" off of his or her ministry, church, home, and personal life. In fact, these same qualities will enable any believer to rise to a new level. God wants us to experience His goodness in all areas! Those who learn

how to utilize the *Barnabas Factor* no longer limit themselves—the sky literally becomes the limit! They become confident that indeed all things are possible to them because they believe! (See Mark 9:23.)

In the previous chapter we discussed how remarkable it was that Barnabas sought the help of Paul during the Antioch revival and how that decision did much to sustain the move of God. Because Barnabas was secure in the Lord, he did not fall prey to any of the attitudes that are common in Christian leaders who are insecure and performance driven. In this chapter we will focus on how leaders treat others, especially those within his or her own ministry. We begin by referring to the same text as the one we used in the previous chapter.

> For a whole year Barnabas and Saul met with the church [at Antioch] and taught great numbers of people. The disciples were called Christians first at Antioch.
>
> Acts 11:26

Barnabas' decision to bring Paul into the leadership of the revival proved to be the right one. For a solid year the pair taught the "great numbers" of people who were born again during the outpouring of God's Spirit. As a result of their excellent teaching and their training of the new converts, the believers became known as *Christians* for the first time. The literal meaning of the word is "one who resembles Christ," meaning that the Gentile believers bore such good fruit that the unbelieving population considered them to be just like Christ, or "little Christs" as some have said! Imagine that! With a testimony like this, it is no wonder that the revival at Antioch was so successful.

God Is the Source

Again I ask the question: why do so many of our modern-day revivals fizzle out? I believe a great deal has to do with the how the leaders treat people. I will explain.

It is unfortunate, but Christian ministry is not all preaching and teaching. Christian leaders need money to live just as lay people do, and often their God-given visions require substantial financial backing. The pressure associated with this can be immense and all consuming. If leaders have not settled the issue that God is the Source for all financial supply, they will be tempted to look to people. Whether it's the Christian business owner giving preferential treatment to certain clients or a missionary pandering to a supporter with deep pockets, showing favoritism does not reflect the fruit of faith and love. This temptation is not a new one. James commented on it:

> As believers in our glorious Lord Jesus Christ, don't show favoritism. Suppose a man comes into your meeting wearing a gold ring and fine clothes, and a poor man in shabby clothes also comes in. If you show special attention to the man wearing fine clothes and say, "Here's a good seat for you," but say to the poor man, "You stand there" or "Sit

on the floor by my feet," have you not discriminated among yourselves and become judges with evil thoughts?

James 2:1–4

When God is our Source of financial supply, we are then free to treat all people with dignity and respect. In God's eyes, the little grandmother who faithfully gives a mere five dollars a month is equally as important as the wealthiest donor. Love sees all people the same.

On the other hand, we are not to be intimidated by the wealthy and successful. There is sometimes a false perception that people of means do not have needs; however, people are people. The affluent need ministry and genuine friendship just as much as those at the bottom of the economic ladder do. Refuse to allow insecurities to cause you to shy away from the rich—or anyone for that matter. Jesus did not and neither should we. We should approach all people with genuine love and sincerity of heart, never looking for anything in return.

Leaders and Staff

For the remainder of the chapter, I want to specifically look at the relationship between Christian leaders and their staff. The same principles can be applied in homes and businesses, but here we will concentrate on ministries. When the relationships between Christian leaders and their staffs are healthy and strong, the ministries will be healthy and strong. If those relationships do not receive proper nourishment, the organizations will become sickly and the flow of the Spirit will be hindered. I believe this is a very serious matter to God.

The first area I want to address is in regard to staff salaries. It is a poor testimony that many ministries underpay their workers. In fact it is so common that it is almost expected. If a ministry is struggling financially, that is one thing; but if the head of the ministry is living an extravagant lifestyle while the staff can barely make ends meet, that is just plain wrong. I encourage every leader to read James 5:1–5. This passage indicates that the cries of employees regarding unfair wages reach the ears of the Lord. The injustice opens the door to a curse. Jesus said that "the worker deserves his wages" (Luke 10:7). A "good man," with the fruit of love operating in his or her life will be motivated to pay workers generously. If anything, employees of Christian churches and ministries should be earning top dollar for their respective positions. It would go a long way in enabling staff members to "serve the Lord with gladness" (Ps. 100:2 NASB).

Some will say, *"But, we cannot afford to do that!"*

My response is that you cannot afford *not* to do it! It is simply not right to preach blessings, prosperity, and giving, but pay poverty wages. Could this be one of the things that is holding back the blessings that many are believing for? Generosity should be a part of every aspect of our lives and ministries, not just a quality to be applied to congregations at offering time.

In addition to offering fair salaries, Christian leaders should treat their staff people with respect. I have witnessed boss's treat their customers very well, then turn around and be rude to their employees. Even more appalling, I have observed pastors show great care and concern for their parishioners yet treat the staff disrespectfully. These things ought not be! Leaders will be held accountable for how they treat those whom the Lord has sent to help them. Those who continue to mistreat their people may wake up one morning to find that God has taken away their "talents" and given them to leaders who will appreciate them. A "good man" will affirm the staff and verbalize appreciation. This is a fruit of love.

A Flawed Model

I think it is helpful to understand what I believe is one of the main reasons why some of these relationships are suffering. In short, I believe it is due to a flawed leadership model. Let me explain.

Many years ago I was having a particularly difficult and unpleasant day on my job. I kept thinking to myself, *This seems so familiar. When have I felt this way before?* I racked my brain trying to figure it out. Finally it dawned on me—I had felt the very same emotions when I played sports as I was growing up!

At that point, I had a revelation. I can only speak for men, but the model of leadership for most of us in America is the athletic coach. If you think about it, most boys play sports at some time during their school years. For the boys lacking a father in the home, coaches are likely the only strong male leaders they are ever exposed to. But even if the father is in the home, a young man's coach has a tremendous influence on him. For the young men who join the armed forces, the military provides strong male leadership as well. But even in the best case scenario where the coach or military officer is excellent, in both cases the style of leadership is basically a dictatorship. It is certainly not a democracy! The mentality is, "It is my way or the highway! No questions asked! And, if you don't like it, don't let the door hit you on the way out!"

To me, this explains a lot of what exists in leadership in the Body of Christ today. Of course this is not the attitude of every Christian leader, but I have seen enough of it that I feel compelled to address it. The effect that this negative leadership style has had on believers—particularly ministry employees—is often devastating.

The Best Model

If the sports and military models are flawed, then where can we find the right model? For believers, our model is

Jesus! Can you imagine *Him* treating His followers in the way described above? Certainly not! Yes, He dealt harshly with the Pharisees who were saddling the people with legalism, but that is not how He addressed His loyal followers.

For me, the best summation of the leadership style of Jesus is found in His own words:

> "You know that those who are regarded as rulers of the Gentiles lord it over them, and their high officials exercise authority over them. Not so with you. Instead, whoever wants to become great among you must be your servant, and whoever wants to be first must be slave of all. For even the Son of Man did not come to be served, but to serve, and to give his life as a ransom for many."
>
> Mark 10:42–45

Did you get that? The King of kings and the Lord of lords, who created us and gave us breath, came to *serve!* What an incredible thought! To that King David would say, *"Selah"*— or "Pause, and calmly think of that." In other words, this thought is so amazing that you need to stop and let it sink in. I encourage you to do just that—meditate on Jesus as being the Savior who came to serve you. Doesn't that make you love Him and want to serve Him even more?

The point here is that the leadership style of Jesus is *servant leadership.* He said that if you want to be the greatest in the Kingdom, you must be the least. (Luke 9:48.) If you want to be the first, you must be the last. (Matthew 20:16.) The way to advance in the Kingdom of God is to step back!

This is totally opposite to the way this world and the natural mind operate. The Lord confirms that the ways of the Kingdom of God are vastly different from the ways of man or our culture:

> "My thoughts are not your thoughts, neither are your ways my ways," declares the LORD. "As the heavens are higher than the earth, so are my ways higher than your ways and my thoughts than your thoughts."
>
> Isaiah 55:8–9

Not surprisingly, it requires a major paradigm shift in thinking for most leaders to implement the Jesus model. We must think like Jesus thinks. Paul said it like this:

> Do not conform any longer to the pattern of this world, but be transformed by the renewing of your mind. Then you will be able to test and approve what God's will is—his good, pleasing and perfect will.
>
> Romans 12:2

We know that Jesus always walked in His Father's "good, pleasing, and perfect will," so we understand that His method of leadership is God's perfect design. If we, therefore, desire to accomplish God's perfect will as leaders, we must conform our thinking—renew our minds—to think about leadership like He does. We must "lift the lid" on the way we have done things in the past and step out in faith to follow Jesus' example.

*L*IFT THE *L*ID!

Servant Leadership

The first requirement to operating after the Jesus model is for the leader to become a servant. That is stating the obvious, but in contemporary society, true servants are few and far between. Jesus himself set the example here when He took on the role of a servant and washed the feet of the disciples on the very night of His betrayal. At that time only lowly servants performed this task—certainly not esteemed teachers! That was unheard of! Talk about a paradigm shift! Peter naturally protested, but Jesus insisted that a true leader in the Kingdom of God must be a servant of all.

The result? We know from the Bible that because of Jesus' selfless leadership, the disciples were more than willing to lay down their lives for Him, some even to the point of being martyred. It is safe to say, then, that when today's Christian leaders pattern themselves after Jesus and become servant leaders, loyalty and diligence on the part of the staff will cease to be an issue. This type of selflessness almost always brings out the best in others.

You may be thinking that this concept goes crossways with your personality, that it is contrary to your "love language"[4] or motivational gift. Think about Jesus for a moment. Philippians 2:7 states that "he gave up his divine privileges; he took the humble position of a slave" (NLT). Did you catch that? He *took* the very nature of a slave or a servant! He chose it! He wanted it! I'm sorry, my friend.

There is no valid excuse for a believer not to practice servant leadership as Jesus did—in the home, in the ministry, or in public. It is effective everywhere!

Paul Understood the Jesus Model

The apostle Paul chose to conform his leadership style to that of Jesus, and he left us a vivid description of exactly how he did it:

> Even though I am free of the demands and expectations of everyone, I have voluntarily become a servant to any and all in order to reach a wide range of people: religious, nonreligious, meticulous moralists, loose-living immoralists, the defeated, the demoralized—whoever. I didn't take on their way of life. I kept my bearings in Christ—but I entered their world and tried to experience things from their point of view. I've become just about every sort of servant there is in my attempts to lead those I meet into a God-saved life.
>
> 1 Corinthians 9:19–22 MSG

Paul did not lead by commanding others to follow him and conform to him, as many leaders have throughout history. Instead he exemplified the Jesus model by empathizing with people and serving them. He became amazingly adept at putting himself in the shoes of his audience and presenting the Gospel in a way that the people could relate to. It is hard to imagine anyone not responding positively to a leader like that!

Lift the Lid!

Servant Leadership Today

What are some examples of servant leadership in contemporary society? We do not commonly wash feet as they did in the first century, but we can take time out of our busy schedules to pray for others. We can make the effort to remember people's names. We can visit the sick and prepare meals for those who are unable to do so themselves. We can go out of our way to let our staff or employees know that we appreciate them and the work they are doing. We can ask them about areas of need, then take their hands and pray. We can serve the members of our own families by being as considerate of them as we are of our guests. Servanthood is primarily an attitude, a lifestyle of constantly thinking of ways to bless the people we touch every day.

Obviously in very large organizations, the person at the top is not capable of actually serving every person under his or her command, but the leader can do a great deal to serve those who directly report to him or her. Those individuals should then be encouraged to pass the blessing down the chain of command. The tone is set at the top.

We have touched on this before, but one of the most profound ways a leader can serve is by taking the time and energy to become a mentor to another believer. Barnabas invested himself in Paul, who in turn many years later, mentored young Timothy, who was just beginning in ministry. I believe that God's design for the Body of Christ is that we should always have a Barnabas in our lives to mentor us and a Timothy whom we can disciple. By this constant flow of receiving then giving out then receiving again, the Body can grow as it should.

Whether or not we actually wash one another's feet today is not the issue. The bottom line is that Jesus desires that leaders in the Body of Christ become servants.

Qualities of Servant Leaders

To bring this to a very practical level, let's look at some of the characteristics of servant leaders. Each is an important fruit of the *Barnabas Factor* at work in the believer's life.

Servant leaders encourage their people. We have talked about encouragement before, but I want to specifically address it in regard to leaders and their workers. It amazes me how both Christian and secular leaders find it difficult to praise their subordinates. They want their workers to excel, but they do not want to give them anything to help them to accomplish their respective tasks. Perhaps it goes back to poor leadership models, but just as a football coach berates a player after a fumble, leaders often come down hard on their workers when mistakes are made. But do the employees ever hear compliments for work well done? Certainly issues arise that must be addressed, but this can be done in a way that preserves the dignity of the worker and encourages him or

her to do better the next time. German poet Johann Wolfgang von Goethe once said, "Correction does much, but encouragement does more. Encouragement after censure is as the sun after a shower." Moms and Dads, this works wonders in the home as well!

Given the length of time Paul worked under the leadership of Barnabas, there is no doubt that Paul made mistakes, which Barnabas had to address. I am confident, though, that the Son of Encouragement administered correction in such a way that Paul was able to receive it and grow.

Servant leaders relate to their people. We read how Paul empathized with the people he led to the Lord, and wise leaders follow his example by making it a point to see things from their people's point of view. Instead of the we/they mentality that so often exists between ministry leaders and their staff, servant leaders bridge the gap. While they maintain their position as leaders, they are not afraid to "get down in the trenches" alongside their workers. Those who lead by intimidation are fearful that if they get too close, their people will lose respect for them and take advantage of the situation. However, just the opposite is true. Leaders who relate to their people, who feel what their support staff feels, who share their frustrations as well as their triumphs, cannot help but be admired.

At least some in the business world have figured this out. I have a nephew-in-law who is employed by one of the Japanese automakers, and he reports that everyone in the company—from the CEO to the janitors—wears the same uniform to work. With that type of team mentality, is it any wonder that Japanese vehicles are synonymous with quality? If something that simple can be so effective in the automobile industry, surely we can come up with creative ideas to build cohesion between leaders and their staffs in our churches and ministries.

This quality is also very effective as parents relate to their children. Whether this means sitting on the floor to play with small children or taking an interest in your teenager's latest hobby, entering your child's world will make you a far more effective—and enjoyable—leader. Teenagers in particular often need to unburden their hearts. It is the wise parent who determines to listen more than to speak, quietly guiding by loving example.

Servant leaders share the credit. Insecure believers are not able to share the credit with others. Say a ministry leader receives praise for exceptional work that was actually done by one of his subordinates. Does he give due credit to the worker? An insecure leader will take all the credit himself. A secure leader, on the other hand, freely acknowledges the hard work of his or her associates and generously praises them. This encourages teamwork and instills pride in the employees for a job well done.

Servant leaders trust their people. We have mentioned that insecure leaders find it hard to trust others, and this definitely affects their management style. The attitude is,

"If you want something done right, you have to do it yourself!" Insecure people are convinced that no one can do a thing better than they can do it; consequently they find it nearly impossible to delegate responsibilities. They are typically micromanagers who are notorious for giving responsibility without the authority to match it.

Jesus, on the contrary, is a great manager of people. He always gives us the authority we need to fulfill the responsibility He has entrusted into our hands. This was clearly evidenced when He gave the Great Commission:

> "All authority in heaven and on earth has been given to me. Therefore go and make disciples of all nations, baptizing them in the name of the Father and of the Son and of the Holy Spirit, and teaching them to obey everything I have commanded you. And surely I am with you always, to the very end of the age."
>
> Matthew 28:18–20

Jesus revealed to His disciples that God had given Him all authority. Notice three characteristics of His managerial style. First, He delegated the authority to His disciples. Next, he laid out their responsibilities—to go, to make disciples of all nations, to baptize, and to teach the new believers to obey Him. Finally, He concluded this charge with the assurance that His presence would be with them everywhere they went! In other words, He would be there to help them.

Jesus does not expect us to win the nations with both hands tied behind our backs. He equips us and helps us. I find it amazing that He is so comfortable trusting us with so much authority. But He knows it is the only way we can achieve our objectives. Christian leaders, in turn, must learn to trust people too.

"But," you may ask, "what if the person fails or makes a mistake?" A secure leader sees failure as merely an opportunity to teach and train the person to do the thing correctly.

Remember that Jesus has entrusted heavenly treasures to "earthen vessels" (2 Cor. 4:7 NASB). The word *earthen* here implies "frailty."[5] In other words, it describes a substance that is so fragile that if it is handled roughly, it will break into a million pieces. We can derive two things from this. The first is that despite how fragile we as humans are, Jesus has entrusted to us a heavenly message along with a divine mandate to take that message to the ends of the earth. He trusts and believes in us, and we as leaders must trust and believe in our people. The second thing we can glean is that earthen vessels must be handled with care. Servant leaders handle their people gently, taking care not to damage them by harsh words or actions. Nowhere is this more critical than in the home where parents have such a major impact on their children's tender emotions.

I have no doubt that when servant leadership is truly implemented and we treat people the way God desires, we will see a big turnaround in churches and ministries. As at Antioch, the Lord will be free to lift the lid for dynamic growth and revival.

Now, looking ahead to the next chapter. Often the Holy Spirit has several things in mind when He moves on us to do something. I believe this was the case when He prompted Barnabas to go to Paul and bring him back to Antioch. It was time for Paul to begin his public ministry in earnest, and what better man to have as his sponsor and co-laborer than Barnabas!

This unselfish move on Barnabas' part proved to be a major step in God's plan to evangelize the world. In fact, the great missionary thrust to the nations gained tremendous impetus as a result of the relationship between Barnabas and Paul. Paul's time at Antioch became the springboard to his destiny—to become an apostle to the Gentiles.

Lord, thank You for sending Jesus to us to reveal Your model for Christian leadership. Whether it is in the ministry, in business, or in our homes, help us to renew our minds to Your way of doing things so that our leadership will be effective. Show us ways we can serve the people we lead, our co-workers, and those in our homes. Amen.

CHAPTER 11

What Really Happened?

RETURNING TO OUR NARRATIVE about Barnabas and Paul, we will pick up where we left off with them teaching the great numbers of believers coming into the church at Antioch. The following are highlights of subsequent events involving the two of them:

- The disciples at Antioch sent them to deliver a gift to believers in Judea. (Acts 11:29–30.)

- They then returned to Antioch with John Mark. (Acts 12:25.)

- Next, they embarked on what has come to be known as Paul's first missionary journey. Everywhere they went,

THE *B*ARNABAS FACTOR

large numbers of people turned out to hear the Word of God and to be saved. During this time, Paul's ministry became more and more pronounced. (Acts 13:1–14:25.)

- Upon returning to Antioch, they shared all that God had done among the Gentiles through them. They stayed with the disciples there for "a long time." (Acts 14:26–28.)

- When some men came from Judea teaching that the Gentiles had to be circumcised in order to be saved, Barnabas and Paul were appointed to take up the matter with the elders and apostles in Jerusalem. (Acts 15:1–3.)

- These leaders, known as the Council at Jerusalem, determined that the Gentile believers were not required to follow the Law of Moses. They appointed Silas and Judas (called Barsabbas) to accompany Barnabas and Paul back to Antioch with a letter stating only a few simple restrictions regarding diet and sexual immorality. (Acts 15:4–33.)

- After Judas and Silas returned to Jerusalem, Barnabas and Paul remained in Antioch. (Acts 15:35.)

Jerusalem Council

The impact of Jerusalem Council mentioned above is often minimized, but its conclusions ultimately determined that the

What Really Happened?

Christian faith would become global in its scope and not remain just a small sect within Judaism. After listening to Paul and Barnabas describe all the miracles and the salvations that had occurred among the Gentiles, the apostles in Jerusalem wisely concluded that the new Gentile believers did not have to adopt Jewish culture in order to become followers of Christ. Rather, they could remain within their own culture and worship Jesus in their own culturally distinctive fashion.

A Roman, for instance, did not have to become a Jew in order to follow Jesus, just as today a Guatemalan does not have to become an American in order to be a Christian. No, the Holy Spirit loves to speak through each culture in ways that uniquely connect the individuals within that group.

Needless to say, this was a landmark decision! From the Jerusalem Council, the Good News of Jesus Christ has literally exploded around the world. Today, there are nearly one billion born again believers living in every country on Earth. Had the early Church leaders decided to require the Gentile believers to become circumcised and to observe all of the Levitical Law, they would certainly have hamstrung the growth of the Church among the Gentiles.

Every Thing Was Fine, Until...

Following the Jerusalem Council, the relational bond between Barnabas and Paul was as strong as ever. In fact

THE *B*ARNABAS FACTOR

after they returned to Antioch, they resumed their ministry to the people there. After a time, a stirring rose up in Paul to follow up on the churches he and Barnabas had planted on their missionary journey. Barnabas evidently agreed. Things were flowing along smoothly until Barnabas announced that he wanted to take John Mark with them. At this point Paul balked!

What occurred next is one of the most disturbing events recorded in the book of Acts—the sharp disagreement and subsequent separation between Paul and Barnabas before what is commonly referred to as Paul's second missionary journey. What happened? How could these two great men of God have allowed such a tragedy after having shared so many remarkable experiences through their ministry together?

Let's first read the account and then attempt to determine the answer.

> Some time later [while in Antioch] Paul said to Barnabas, "Let us go back and visit the brothers in all the towns where we preached the word of the Lord and see how they are doing." Barnabas wanted to take John, also called Mark, with them, but Paul did not think it wise to take him, because he had deserted them in Pamphylia and had not continued with them in the work.[6] They had such a sharp disagreement that they parted company. Barnabas took Mark and sailed for Cyprus, but Paul chose Silas and left, commended by the brothers to the grace of the Lord. He went through Syria and Cilicia, strengthening the churches.
>
> Acts 15:36–41

What Really Happened?

Silent Treatment?

Interestingly, Barnabas is never mentioned again in the book of Acts! If you will remember from earlier in this book we offered several explanations for the shift in focus from Barnabas to Paul.[7] However, many commentators conclude that this is proof that God sided with Paul on this issue with Mark. They believe that the silence is a sort of judgment on Barnabas. But if that were true, we would have to deduce that Peter was also judged because he is not mentioned again in Acts either!

What saddens me the most about this conclusion is that it has blinded so many to the incredible impact that Barnabas and his ministry had on the early Church. He may not have been mentioned again in Acts, but his influence remained positive. In fact, Paul himself mentioned Barnabas in Galatians 2:1, 9; 1 Corinthians 9:6; and Colossians 4:10—the latter two being written *after* their split over Mark!

Another reason that I do not believe that Luke, the writer of Acts, disliked Barnabas or that he used "the silent treatment" as his commentary on the split is based on his description of Barnabas as a "good man, full of the Holy Spirit and faith" (Acts 11:24). Although Luke may or may not have known Barnabas personally, it is highly unlikely that he would have written of him in such positive terms had he not believed this about Barnabas.

Another plausible explanation as to why Luke became silent about Barnabas after the split has to do with the Council at Jerusalem mentioned above and written about in Acts 15. It was at that meeting that the landmark decision was made that the Gospel could be taken to the Gentiles (nations). Prior to this time, the focus had been on the Jews receiving salvation and being filled with the Holy Spirit. With this tremendous paradigm shift toward the Gentiles, it is quite logical for Luke's focus to shift in that direction as well. Since Paul was called to be the Apostle to the Gentiles, naturally his ministry would be the one highlighted. Peter, on the other hand, was known as the Apostle to the Jews, which could explain why he is no longer mentioned in Acts.

Incidentally, this focus on reaching the nations should be the focus of all believers. If you will notice, the book of Acts does not have a conclusion; it is open ended. I believe that is because chapters are still being added today!

Back to the Main Issue

Unfortunately, the split between Barnabas and Paul has received so much attention that the most important issue, in my opinion, has been overlooked. That is why I have taken so much time to "debunk" much of the speculation regarding Barnabas. Now, let us go back to the incident that caused the split in the first place.

What Really Happened?

If you remember, Mark accompanied Barnabas and Paul on what came to be known as Paul's first missionary journey. For reasons unknown, Mark suddenly "left them to return to Jerusalem" (Acts 13:13). The main issue in my opinion and as it pertains to our study of the *Barnabas Factor* is that Barnabas wanted to give Mark a second chance, but Paul was not willing to.

At this point in his life, Paul no doubt operated under the premise of "Burn me once, and it is your fault. Burn me twice, and it is my fault." Mark had failed them once when they needed him, and Paul was not going to give him the opportunity to do it to him again. Barnabas, the encourager, on the other hand, looked at this differently. He saw potential, no doubt, in Mark and was willing to give him a second chance, once again proving himself to be a risk taker.

It is amazing how many people share Paul's attitude: "If you fail me once, you will never get a second chance." It happens in the Church, in the home, at school, and at the workplace. When I witness this, I often think about how thankful I am that Jesus does not have this attitude toward us. He never gives up on us regardless of how many times we fail Him. Why, then, can we not do the same for others? Is Jesus not our example? Remember, failure in others is always an opportunity to teach; we should never view it as an end.

Two Teams Are Better than One

Evidently, both Paul and Barnabas felt so strongly about their convictions in this matter that they split into two teams. Paul took Silas and headed back to Asia Minor, while Barnabas and Mark sailed for Cyprus. The upside of this is that there were now two missionary teams spreading the Gospel rather than one; but splits are never pleasant, no matter how we try to rationalize them. There is often collateral damage as innocent people get hurt.

Who was right in this disagreement between Paul and Barnabas? The event is never mentioned again in Scripture, but we can reach some conclusions, based on what we know about Mark's subsequent life. The first thing is that Mark later authored the gospel that bears his name. According to Bible scholars, his was the first gospel written, and Matthew and Luke used it as a pattern to write their own, the three together forming what is known as the Synoptic Gospels. We also know that Mark served as Peter's assistant for some time and that Mark's gospel was written from Peter's perspective.[8]

A final conclusion about Mark can be deduced from a rather obscure verse in Paul's final letter:

> Only Luke is with me. Get Mark and bring him with you, because he is helpful to me in my ministry.
>
> 2 Timothy 4:11

What Really Happened?

Did you catch that? Paul instructed Timothy to bring *Mark* when he came to see him because he considered Mark helpful in the ministry! This is the same Mark who had split the missionary team many years earlier, and now Paul wanted to see him. Quite a switch from his previous attitude! Obviously much had transpired in the lives of both Paul and Mark—forgiveness and reconciliation, to name two.

So what happened to Mark between Acts 15 and 2 Timothy 4? We can only surmise that Barnabas had a substantial influence on him during their time together. Mark obviously continued to mature in his Christian walk to become a quality, faithful servant of the Lord.

Thank God for secure leaders who never give up their protégées! Everyone needs someone to believe in him or her like Barnabas believed in Mark. How many Marks have slipped through the Church because they were cast aside for making mistakes? What could have taken place in Church history had there been more people like Barnabas to help the young Marks recover, to see the potential in them and mentor them so that they could fulfill their destiny? We may never know, but we can strive to follow Barnabas' example and work to restore those who fall.

Unsung Hero

I think it is important for us to realize that Barnabas was indirectly responsible for much of the New Testament we enjoy today. It was he who took the risk to meet Paul and to validate his life and ministry with the church leaders in Jerusalem. It was he who sought out Paul in Tarsus and mentored him for ministry in Antioch. It was he who gave Mark the second chance and mentored him for ministry as well. Think of what we would have missed out on had he not cared enough to go the extra mile with these two! Paul wrote over half of the New Testament and Mark wrote the first gospel! These are the reasons why I believe that Barnabas is one of the greatest leaders in the New Testament.

As we have stated many times before, secure believers are fruitful, and Barnabas was certainly that. They have an insatiable desire to obey the Lord and to accomplish His will in the earth. They do not seek fame, and they do not care who gets the credit. This could be another explanation for the silence toward Barnabas toward the end of Acts. Knowing what we do about him, we can safely assume that he was not a self-promoting individual. I doubt it even fazed him that he was not getting all of the press.

Remember: secure leaders are fruitful and do not care who gets the credit as long as Jesus gets the glory. Some commentators have even suggested that Barnabas wrote the book of Hebrews, although no one knows with certainty who wrote it. If indeed Barnabas was the writer, it would have been typical for him not to put his name on the book so that the focus would be on Jesus instead of on him.

What Really Happened?

The fact is, the landscape of Church history is dotted with men and women whom few have ever heard of, but you can rest assured that they are well known in heaven. What we do may go unnoticed by others, but unselfish faithfulness on our part does not get past the Lord. He will reward us in due season.

In this present hour, there is a crying need for more leaders like Barnabas who will look for the Pauls and the Marks to mentor for leadership. There is a prophetic mandate, if you will, on this present generation of young people to complete the Great Commission, and more mentors like Barnabas are needed to train them. This is why it is so vital that we develop our security in the Lord. It is the only way that we can pass on this legacy to the next generation and break the cycle of insecurity.

People Oriented versus Task Oriented

A pastor friend of mine, Phil T. Dunn, uses the disagreement between Paul and Barnabas to help him to choose the right person when hiring a new member for his pastoral staff. He asks the candidate who he or she thinks is correct, Paul or Barnabas. The answer reveals whether the applicant is task oriented like Paul or people-oriented like Barnabas. Pastor Phil wisely understands that ministers need to have a genuine love for people and be willing to work with their shortcomings and mistakes.

I tell pastors all over the world that if their people had no problems, then there would be no need for them. That is why we are in the ministry. We are called to shepherd the sheep and to deal with the problems just as Barnabas did with Mark.

If you think about it, this is true for parents as well. If our children never made mistakes and automatically knew everything, there would be no need for parents. Training, discipling, and mentoring are all reasons that parents are necessary. When children make poor choices, they do not need to be yelled at, but rather lovingly corrected and taught. We must be especially mindful of this so that we do not pass on a spirit of insecurity, for it will grow worse for each subsequent generation. This is why it is imperative that we deal with the identity issue. A lack of security does not just impact our lives, but it directly affects everyone around us, whether we want to admit it or not.

Paul's Transformation

Even though Paul may have been more task oriented early in his ministry, I believe he mellowed to become a man who genuinely loved people and put them first—true evidence of a secure leader. Three passages of Scripture point to his remarkable transformation as he matured to become all God intended him to become:

What Really Happened?

- In the final chapter of Romans, one of his latter epistles, his love for people and the emphasis he placed on relationships is pronounced. In the first sixteen verses, he mentioned nearly thirty people by name, individually affirming what each one meant to him. He was affectionate and grateful to others throughout the chapter as well, even singling out women, which was quite rare for his day.

- Although he had every reason to be proud from a natural standpoint, Paul developed a truly humble spirit over the course of his ministry, eventually coming to the realization that all of his accomplishments and accolades were meaningless in comparison to knowing Christ! (Phil. 3:4–11.) He realized that it was not all about him and his ministry, but all about Jesus. And Jesus is all about people.

- Again reflecting his genuine love for others, Paul wrote, "What is it we [Paul, Sylvanus, and Timothy] live for, that gives us hope and joy and is our proud reward and crown? It is you! Yes, you will bring us much joy as we stand together before our Lord Jesus Christ when he comes back again. For you are our trophy and joy" (1 Thess. 2:19–20 TLB). Paul did not look forward to trophies for his accomplishments, education, ministry, or bank account. His crown and joy was people!

Who else does that remind you of? The writer of Hebrews said:

> Let us fix our eyes on Jesus, the author and perfecter of our faith, who *for the joy set before him* endured the cross, scorning its shame, and sat down at the right hand of the throne of God.
>
> v. 12:2 (emphasis added)

It was for the joy set before him that Jesus went to the cross and endured the pain and shame. What joy? I believe he was talking about you and me! *We* are His joy; *we* are the reason He went to the cross! Paul cultivated this heart for people, and we, too, should allow the Spirit of Jesus to be developed in our individual lives.

Excuses, Excuses

Many people use the excuse that they are naturally wired tightly or that their personality is task oriented. They claim it is the way God made them and that they cannot change. Translation: that usually means that they do not want to change even if it means becoming more fruitful and obedient to the Lord.

Early in his ministry, Paul might have said the same, but look at the changes that took place in his life. No, I do not believe that we should use our personalities as an excuse. We may have a tendency to be more one way or the other

because of our environment, upbringing, or natural temperament, but through the transforming work of the Holy Spirit in our lives, we can all become more like Jesus. If you struggle in this area, allow Paul's example to inspire you!

Once our identity is properly placed in Christ, then His attributes will manifest in our lives. I know this to be true because it has happened in my own life. When I began in ministry, I was fairly task oriented and rather hard on people; however, when the Holy Spirit began to deal with my identity issue, I began to view people differently. Over the course of several years of dealing with people on a regular basis, I began to realize that there are no pat answers. I became more merciful and able to extend grace to all people. Thanks to the work of the Holy Spirit, I changed—and you can too.

A Healthy Balance

Allow me to add that I try to strike a healthy balance between accomplishing tasks and developing relationships. If I err one way or the other, however, I believe it should be toward relationships. For instance, I will sacrifice the task if it will negatively affect a relationship with another person. I will not, however, sacrifice a relationship to accomplish a task. People come first! (See, Rom. 14:13; 1 Cor. 8:13)

With that in mind, I would like to say a word about ministries in particular. I have heard it said that a ministry should be run in a business-like manner, but it cannot be run like a business. Why? Because the bottom line for a ministry is people—not a profit margin. I firmly believe that if people are put first—both the target audience of the ministry as well as the people who are employed by the ministry—the bottom line will take care of itself. The business people to whom I have spoken confirm the wisdom in this concept. They all agree that even in the business world if you put people first, it will boost your profit margin.

When dealing with the nuts and bolts of running a ministry, it is understandable that the focus can easily shift to finances. After all, it takes money to operate. We cannot forget, however, that our main task is to reach, touch, and love people—for it is then that we truly reflect the heart of Jesus.

Flying Solo

In the book of Acts, an excellent strategy was implemented that I think is crucial today. As the Church began sending apostolic teams to crisscross the known world with the Gospel, both Paul and Barnabas always traveled in teams. Even after their split, each took another traveling companion. Silas accompanied Paul, and Mark traveled with

What Really Happened?

Barnabas. They rarely ever traveled alone. Why? There are countless reasons, but I want to highlight one in particular.

First let me state that it takes a secure man or woman to bring another person on board. Working as a team involves crucifying the flesh in order to share the leadership and the credit. It is much easier at times to fly solo, but the danger of giving in to momentary temptation is greatly increased. I can assure you that none of the leaders in Acts fell prey to the traps that so many of our leaders fall into today. Of course there are times when traveling alone becomes unavoidable, but because it is so risky, it should be the exception and not the rule.

I learned of a prime example of this from my good friend Greg Ford, founder and president of Global Quest Ministries and Sudan for Christ. In the mid-1990s, he took a team of leaders to Cuba to minister. One day while on Isla de Juventud (the Isle of Youth), Greg noticed a beautiful, scantly-clad, Cuban girl walking around the hotel pool. The thought occurred to him that she was probably working the hotel as a prostitute.

Later, when he returned to his room, his roommate had quite a story to tell! He said that he heard a knock at the door while he was taking a shower. Expecting it to be Greg, he wrapped a towel around his waist and went to answer the door. When he opened it, this same young senorita was standing there with an enticing smile on her face asking him for a drink of water. He immediately responded with a negative and slammed the door shut.

It was a demonic setup, but thank God this man was able to resist it. The fact that he was not traveling alone made it that much easier to respond appropriately. Think about the situation for a moment. He was far from home and what she was offering is widely accepted in Cuba. On top of that, with virtually no contact between the people of Cuba and the United States, he could have enjoyed a fling and no one except God would have ever known. I am not insinuating that this particular man would have given in to this temptation, but I am saying that because he was a part of a team of ministers, it was much easier to resist the senorita's advances.

Isolation is one of the devil's most effective tools in trying to defeat us. I have heard it said that isolation breeds desolation. That is one of the many reasons it is so vital that we stay in fellowship with other believers. (Hebrews 10:25.)

Sad to say, I have heard of circumstances where ministers traveling alone in other countries have not been able to overcome the loneliness and the temptations. In fact, I have even heard of one minister who contracted AIDS as a result of a one-time encounter on the mission field. In this day and age, we need to ensure that we live above reproach and that we protect the name of Jesus.

The Devil's Plan Was Thwarted

Thankfully the disagreement between Barnabas and Paul did not stop the work of the ministry. As big of a challenge as their split must have been, it was not the only event that threatened to derail their ministry and stop the spread of the Gospel around the world. We will discuss another potentially devastating incident in the next chapter.

Lord, help all of us in the Body of Christ to accomplish our necessary tasks but to always make people our first priority. Remind us not to "shoot our own wounded" when our fellow believers fall but to reach out in compassion and restore them. Help us, also, to continue adding chapters to the book of Act by winning the nations to Jesus as they did in the early Church. Amen.

CHAPTER 12

Champions for Christ

CHAMPIONS. WE REVERE THEM, admire them, and even dream of becoming champions ourselves. In this chapter we will look at a couple of great champions for Christ and the qualities that made them so.

When it comes to sports, we all understand that for a person to become a champion it requires talent, hard work, self-discipline, mental toughness, and good coaching. But even if an athlete has all of these things going for him or her, to become a champion requires one other essential quality—a champion *never quits*. Even in the face of defeat or failure, the champion musters the courage and determination to keep on going. It is this quality that separates the champion from the rest of the pack.

How many times do you think gymnast Mary Lou Retton, gold-medal winner at the 1984 Los Angeles Olympics, fell off the balance beam before she perfected the skill? Or, how many times did Pelé, the famous Brazilian soccer player, miss goals before he became one of the greatest soccer players in the world? Or, how many times did Michael Jordan miss shots in basketball before he became arguably the greatest basketball player to ever play the game? The answer in all three cases is *countless* times! Each probably missed more goals than they made over their respective athletics careers, but they are all still considered world champions.

Failure—and even success, for that matter—is not the true test of a champion. The true test of a champion is in what he or she does after failure. *Champions don't quit*—which is another important characteristic of the *Barnabas Factor*. Those who are secure in Christ understand that no matter how bleak a situation seems, there is always hope in God. Instead of giving up in frustration, they somehow find a way to rise, dust themselves off, and press on toward the goal of perfecting their skills or winning the prize of their heavenly calling.

We have all missed our goals, made mistakes, and failed in one way or another, but that is not the main issue. I believe the major emphasis should be placed on what we do *after* we stumble. A true champion tenaciously keeps going, no matter how many failures line the path. Let the same be said of you. No matter what, keep on plugging because "God … always causeth us to triumph in Christ" (2 Cor. 2:14 KJV).

As far as champions for Christ go, the apostle Paul heads the list. What was his secret for success? He told us in his own words:

> Forgetting what is behind and straining toward what is ahead, I press on toward the goal to win the prize for which God has called me heavenward in Christ Jesus.
>
> Philippians 3:13–14

No matter what came against him, Paul put it behind him and kept going till he met Jesus face to face. As I have stated in a previous chapter, others do not remember how quickly you start; they only remember how strong you finish. The Christian life is a long-distance race, and you must persevere until you reach the finish line and hear the words, "Well done, My good and faithful servant!" (Matt. 25:23.) It does not matter what happens, what others do or do not do to you, or who lets you down. You must press on toward the finish line and not quit until you reach it. Athletic champions persevere for a trophy that will ultimately fade and perish. How much more should we strive for crowns that will never perish! (1 Cor. 9:25.)

THE BARNABAS FACTOR

Barnabas, the Champion for Jesus

I have mentioned before that I believe Barnabas was one of the greatest leaders in the New Testament. He was also, without a doubt, a true champion for Christ. But he was not without faults—which should give us all hope. The thing that makes him a champion in my book is that he did not give up when others might have. Let's look at the following passage, and then I will explain.

> When Peter came to Antioch, I opposed him to his face, because he was clearly in the wrong. Before certain men came from James, he used to eat with the Gentiles. But when they arrived, he began to draw back and separate himself from the Gentiles because he was afraid of those who belonged to the circumcision group. The other Jews joined him in his hypocrisy, so that by their hypocrisy *even Barnabas was led astray.*
>
> Galatians 2:11–13 (emphasis added)

I realize that according to this passage, Paul only addressed Peter to the face; but, verse 14 goes on to say that this confrontation took place "in front of them all." Since Barnabas was one of the leaders there, most likely he was one of the ones present. But even if he wasn't present at that very moment, no doubt he received the message loud and clear. The key issue for our discussion is how Barnabas dealt with this failure. Let's begin by examining the context of this situation.

More than likely this confrontation occurred right after Barnabas and Paul had returned from delivering an offering to Jerusalem but before the two began their first missionary journey. (See Acts 11:27–30; 12:25; 13:1–3.) From this, we can safely conclude that even though Barnabas blew it, he did not give up. Shortly after this confrontation, he and Paul began the missions thrust of their ministry together. In fact the greatest days of his ministry were yet to come.

Barnabas' ability to put this incident behind him and go forward in his calling is one of the key factors that makes him a champion in my estimation. Imagine the remorse he must have felt when he realized the pain he had caused his Gentile brothers and sisters. Surely they had felt betrayed. An insecure person would have wallowed in guilt and condemnation, feeling unworthy to continue in ministry. But because Barnabas was secure in the Lord, he knew God would forgive him the moment he confessed his error. He was also able to forgive himself, which is often the hardest thing of all. But because Barnabas kept his end goal in sight, he persevered. We must not give in to discouragement either, but learn from our mistakes and press on.

What's All the Fuss About?

What was Paul so upset about? We can only surmise some of the details, but here is the most probable scenario. Peter no doubt wanted to witness firsthand the incredible revival among the Gentiles in Antioch, so he may have traveled with Barnabas and Paul back to Antioch after the two had delivered the offering from the church at Antioch to the Jerusalem church. When Peter first arrived, it appears that he ate with the Gentiles and even shared the same house with some of them.

According to Jewish laws and customs, this was not a very kosher thing for him to do. Jewish people of that day did not enter the homes of Gentiles, and they certainly did not eat with them. But in the first instance of instant replay ever recorded in history, three times God had revealed to Peter in a vision that He did not differentiate between Jews and Gentiles. That combined with the subsequent events that took place at the house of Cornelius, a Gentile, indicated that the barrier between the two groups of people had been torn down. (See Acts 10:9–11:18.)

Everything was going well in Antioch between Peter and the new Gentile converts. As one of the disciples who had been closest to Jesus, he had much to share with them about the Savior. Their fellowship was warm and joyful. Then, some Jewish believers arrived from Jerusalem who began to make a mess of things by stirring up confusion.

Paul referred to these Orthodox Jews as "Judaizers" because they insisted that the Gentiles had to first obey the Jewish law of circumcision before they could become Christians. In other words, they added requirements to salvation rather that it being by faith alone.

We are not told why Peter did this, but when the Judaizers arrived, he began to disassociate himself with the Gentile believers and began to socialize exclusively with the Jewish believers. Peter's example influenced other Jewish believers to do the same—including Barnabas.

Perhaps in Peter's mind, he was keeping the peace. Or maybe he feared he would lose favor or respect with the Judaizers. He knew they would become highly offended if they saw him fraternizing with the Gentile believers. Maybe he had planned to resume fellowship with the Gentiles after the Judaizers left, hoping that the Gentiles would not become too upset in the meantime. Whatever his reasons, Peter tried to take the path of least resistance, but it did not work. His hypocrisy was soon exposed!

The Confrontation

Evidently, the Gentiles were offended by Peter's actions, and Paul felt the need to confront the two-faced behavior, which he did with about as much tact as a bull in a china shop! Imagine the scene as Paul dressed down Peter in front of all the other believers.

Now, I do not usually recommend publicly correcting people—especially in regard to correcting a leader—but I believe Paul felt the need to confront this situation in this way because of the far-reaching implications of it. If he did not nip this segregation in the bud, it could have greatly hindered the spread of the Gospel among the Gentiles. The fact that he was willing to confront this issue at all indicates that Paul was a very secure individual.

Insecure people usually avoid confrontation until they are forced to deal with a matter. By then, the situation is often so bad that the person explodes, creating a new set of problems. Secure people, on the other hand, are not afraid to confront because they love people and know the benefits of dealing with shortcomings. They realize that if left alone, sin will grow and affect many people. If dealt with early, however, much pain can be avoided.

It is important to remember that the goal should always be to correct, not embarrass. That is why I do not recommend publicly correcting others in most instances. It has been my observation that those who publicly correct others are not necessarily doing it because they are concerned about the truth or right and wrong. Usually their goal is to be seen and heard and to garner support for their view. If you have an issue with someone—especially if the person is a leader—go to the person in private. Then, armed with a heart of humility and love and a tactful manner, bring the matter to the person's attention. It takes a much stronger and more secure individual to confront in love, but the one who does will have a much better chance of being received.

Secure people are in control of their emotions and the situation when they need to confront an issue. I find that the "Sandwich Principle" helps things to go more smoothly. A sandwich consists of some sort of filling, flanked by a slice of bread on each side. Likewise every negative behavior to be confronted should be sandwiched between two affirmations. This requires planning on your part, but it will make the issue much easier to swallow. And remember, a secure person is never vindictive but always has restoration as the goal.

A Team of Advisers

Over the years I have been perplexed with the inability that seemingly quality leaders have in dealing with negative issues. Many are not at all accustomed to being corrected, especially if they have insulated themselves with "yes men"—those who will only tell the leader what they think he or she wants to hear. When this type of leader is confronted, he or she will likely display anger and react in a fashion unbecoming to a Christian leader. This is actually a very dangerous place for a leader because "yes men" lack the courage to warn of foreseen dangers. When a ship is headed for disaster, the man on the lookout warns the captain to change course. But many subordinates are afraid to speak the truth for fear of being accused of having a bad attitude or being reprimanded or fired. Leaders need to assure those under their leadership that they will not be penalized if they speak up when they see trouble ahead.

I highly recommend that leaders surround themselves with people who think like they do as well as others who, because of their temperament and background, bring an additional vantage point to the table, individuals who can contribute views that the leader might not see otherwise. Healthy, secure leaders are not threatened by differing viewpoints and can handle it when their people disagree with their ideas. And this is the kind of leader the Body of Christ needs, because there will be times when the leader must make tough decisions. Only one with this kind of backbone can take an unpopular stand when it is the right thing to do.

Solomon, one of the greatest leaders of all time, gave us an excellent word regarding this:

> The wise are mightier than the strong,
> and those with knowledge grow stronger and stronger.
> So don't go to war without wise guidance;
> victory depends on having many advisers.
>
> Proverbs 24:5–6 NLT

I believe the kind of advisers that this passage is talking about are those who will look at the leader's ideas and vision from all vantage points. I learned from a very good friend of mine—Jerry Williamson, President of Calvary International Missions—that a healthy ministry needs three groups of people working harmoniously together:

Visionaries—those who see the big picture and have creative ideas. Most leaders of organizations are visionaries.

The downside is that often they are not very practical, only seeing the goal and not understanding what it takes to reach it. Visionaries are also notorious for not giving adequate attention to timing. In their zeal they often do not want to wait for the time it takes to properly cast the vision to others. This can make for a very frustrated staff.

Structural people—the planners and detail/administrative people who keep the vision on track. The negative side is that they often have large policy manuals. Projects are accomplished but usually very slowly. If there is a problem, for example, they want to add a new policy and another layer of leadership to deal with it. This has a tendency to bog things down. Some call it *bureaucracy*.

Relationship people—those who are more concerned about the process than the goal. They want to make sure people are not being used and abused. This is noble, and surprisingly it is a concern that is all too often absent among Christian organizations. The downside, however, of a ministry with only relationship-oriented people is that in spite of the fact that everyone is happy, nothing much is accomplished.

What is needed is a well-balanced team with representatives from each group who are encouraged to bring their strengths to the table. With the proper give and take, these groups will balance one another and form a cohesive unit. The secure leader will neither be threatened by the successes of subordinates nor offended by differences of opinion, and the result will be a healthy, dynamic organization.

Can You Receive Correction?

Returning to our narrative about Paul correcting Peter and Barnabas over the issue of segregation, I want to bring out another significant factor regarding Barnabas' response. We discussed before that Barnabas did not get discouraged and quit the ministry. He repented and went on. But how did this incident affect his relationship with Paul? After all, Barnabas was the mentor and Paul the protégé. We are not told specifically, but based on the fact that the pair continued to work together, Barnabas obviously did not allow the incident to drive a wedge between them. Instead of being offended by Paul and getting into strife, Barnabas humbly accepted the correction, kept his heart right, and did not let it affect their relationship adversely.

This points to one of the fruits of secure people—they can receive correction from others even if it is not given in the right spirit or at the proper time. They can even receive it from peers and subordinates. King Solomon is considered to be the wisest man who ever lived. One thing that made him wise was that no matter how much it hurt, he listened to the counsel of those around him.

> If you listen to constructive criticism,
> you will be at home among the wise.
> If you reject discipline, you only harm yourself;
> but if you listen to correction, you grow in understanding.
>
> Proverbs 15:31–32 NLT

Only the humble and those who are secure in the Lord are able to walk in this level maturity.

Timely Advice, Valid Criticism

Not only did Solomon understand the importance of receiving correction, he also understood the fine art of delivering it.

> Timely advice is as lovely as golden apples in a silver basket. Valid criticism is as treasured by the one who heeds it as jewelry made from finest gold.
>
> Proverbs 25:11–12 NLT (96)

In order for advice to be well received, it must consist of two qualities: it must be timely and it must be valid. Wisdom determines whether or not the knowledge that you possess is necessary for the need at the moment. Discretion understands that there is a time to speak and there is a time to stay quiet. These are good things to keep in mind whenever offering advice, but never is it more critical than when delivering it to a leader.

I have witnessed situations where people have tried to correct a pastor about a matter right before he enters the pulpit to preach. Believe it or not, I have even seen this take place in the middle of a church service! That is always a bad move. Even though most of us have more discretion than that, it illustrates the point.

It is important to note that what we are talking about here is *constructive* criticism, not *destructive* criticism. If your goal is motivated by sincere love and a genuine desire for the betterment of the individual, then it will more than likely be *constructive*. If you think about it, *constructive* means to build up or to edify. This should be our goal. On the other hand, if your correction is motivated by impure intentions such as anger or spite, then you run the risk of giving *destructive criticism*. Ask yourself, *What is the purpose in giving this advice? What are my motives?* People can always justify their actions, but mature believers are completely honest with themselves. They do not spiritualize matters to disguise fleshly motives. When in doubt, wait until your heart is clear.

Understand the Source

Hard medicine is never easy to take, but one thing that worked in Paul's favor—in regard to the confrontation in Galatians 2:11–21—was that Barnabas knew him well. They had shared a longstanding, trusting relationship; and despite

Paul's gruff delivery, Barnabas knew that his partner in ministry loved and respected him. He knew where Paul was coming from, so to speak. This made it much easier for him to receive the correction. In the same way, we must share a history with any person we correct. Otherwise, we are wasting our breath.

Because these two knew one another so well, Barnabas also understood Paul's personality. Paul had a strong spirit, and early on in his ministry he probably did not possess much finesse in dealing with people. This may be the reason he dealt with this issue of hypocrisy with such gruffness. As we have seen, Paul eventually became much more relational in his approach to believers,[9] and it stands to reason that he also softened his manner when it came to administering correction. I do, however, give Paul the benefit of doubt in Galatians, because he obviously felt this issue was so important that he needed to deal with it openly and head on. After all, this issue did impact the entire future of the Church. No small matter indeed!

Where the Rubber Meets the Road

This whole issue of giving and receiving correction is one area where the rubber really meets the road where a person's security is concerned. The proud and arrogant despise correction. Anytime you see someone who cannot receive criticism, you know that have an insecure person on your hands. An angry reaction is an indication that the individual's root system is diseased or malnourished.

A humble spirit, on the other hand, indicates a healthy root system. Secure people actually welcome correction from people who have their best interest at heart. But even when the person is acting out of wrong motives, secure leaders will try to understand where the person is coming from rather than become offended. They can see past fleshly attitudes and even an insulting tone of voice and listen to the content of what is said. Proverbs tells us that, "a fool is quick-tempered, but a wise person stays calm when insulted" (v. 12:16 NLT). The wise do not just "blow off" criticism, regardless of how it is given, but will give is prayerful consideration. After all, it may be valid.

That being said, there is a right way and a wrong way to offer constructive criticism. When corrected wrongly, the wise, secure leader will use the situation to teach the subordinate how to correct according to the fruit of the Spirit. When self-control, love, and kindness dictate motive, attitude, timing, and manner, even the toughest medicine can be received.

Iron Sharpens Iron

This brings up the issue of *accountability*. Barnabas and Paul, more than likely, had a strong accountable relationship with each other. They were probably used to correcting and encouraging each other in their walk with God and in their ministry gifts. Again, Solomon put it aptly:

> As iron sharpens iron, so one man sharpens another.
> Proverbs 27:17

I love this analogy because if you have ever seen two pieces of metal strike one another this way, you know that sparks fly. Likewise, when two people come together to keep each other accountable, sparks may fly when conflict arises. The two, however, must resolve the differences in order for the relationship to work as it should, but their efforts will be rewarded. They will become razor sharp in the hands of the Lord! If you think about it, sin and the influences of the world have a tendency to make us dull spiritually. We need others to help keep us sharp! After all, how do you sharpen metal? By striking it with another piece of metal.

I believe this is why many men especially do not like to be held accountable. They do not like the sparks and the confrontation and will avoid it at all costs. Pride and machismo are often our downfall. Men are afraid to open up and to become vulnerable to other men because they fear rejection and betrayal. This inability to be transparent with others is, as I am sure you can see, a fruit of insecurity.

Secure believers, on the other hand, see the need for relationships in which they can be held accountable. Is there a person in your life, other than your spouse, who is of the same gender, whom you respect spiritually and trust implicitly? In today's environment, it is imperative that you have at least one person whom you have given the right to speak into your life, regardless of the circumstances. If this individual sees any potential weaknesses, he or she has your permission to speak to you about it. In order for this to work as it should, both individuals must be totally transparent. Obviously not just anyone qualifies. It takes time to develop this type of trusting relationship, but it could save your life!

Paul, Barnabas, and Timothy

We have mentioned before that every believer should have a Paul to serve as mentor and a Timothy to disciple. Pastor Sharon Daugherty of Victory Christian Center in Tulsa, Oklahoma, builds upon this idea in her excellent book *Avoiding Deception.* She defines your *Paul* as being someone who is more mature spiritually than you are, someone who can speak into your life. Your pastor is one of your Pauls, and you may have more.

Your *Timothy* is a person you are mentoring. Naturally we pour ourselves into our children, but I have great respect for Christian leaders who mentor young men and women outside their household. Sad to say, this type of mentoring relationship is the exception rather than the norm.

Finally, and most pertinent here, your *Barnabas* is your peer or your accountability partner. As the title of Pastor Sharon's book indicates, this person can help you "avoid deception" as well as other traps of the enemy.

In order for us to live well-rounded, healthy Christian lives, we all need each at least one Paul, one Timothy, and one Barnabas. If you have not already established these kinds of relationships, I urge you to pray for God to lead you to the right people. As you reap the rich rewards that will result, you will be glad you made the effort.

AARP

I want to share more about accountability, so bear with me as I explain how I came to additional understanding on that subject. When I was in my late twenties, my dad took early retirement from his job, and since I am named after him (a junior), I began to receive mail from the American Association for Retired Persons (AARP). It was rather humorous for a young man in his twenties to be receiving mail for retired people. One day while eating breakfast alone, I began to flip through AARP's magazine, *Modern Maturity*. As I did, the Lord began to speak to me in one of those moments when you least expect it. He said that he wanted to teach me the characteristics of a mature Christian leader, and he used the initials *AARP* to do it.

A stands for *Approachable.* Are you approachable? Do people feel comfortable coming up to you? Or, do you have an air about you that gives the impression that you really do not have time to talk to insignificant people? My observation has been that intimidating people, while coming across as very "together," are actually quite insecure, while those who are warm and approachable are much more secure. Interestingly, I have found that this principle holds true for leaders just as much as for those who are not in positions of authority. It is symptomatic of the human condition. Now whenever I see an intimidating person, I wonder to myself, *What is that person hiding behind those intimidating airs?*

We should look to Jesus as our example. Little children approached him freely and even sat on His lap. Adults might press through an intimidating manner, but children will shy away. Jesus was obviously warm and inviting for children to have felt that comfortable around Him. Now the scribes and Pharisees were a different matter. They probably did feel intimidated by Jesus, but for good reason.

How approachable are you? A good way to find out is to watch how children react to you, especially those who are not your own. Fathers, how comfortable are your own children in coming to you with their problems? Do they like to talk to you, or do they have the attitude, "Why bother?" There should always be an open-door policy between your children and you. They need to feel your unconditional acceptance.

The second *A* stands for *Accountable*, pointing to the importance of the accountability relationships we just talked about. Mature leaders—whether they are men or women—recognize this critical need, and it is one of the reasons you rarely see mature leaders fall into sin. They have made themselves accountable.

The men's fellowship Straight Talk for Men in Tulsa, Oklahoma, recommends that accountability partners meet on a weekly basis. The following are some practical questions they suggest that partners pose to one another:

1. Have you been with a person of the opposite sex this last week (other than your spouse) where the instance could have been seen as compromising?
2. Have any of your financial dealings lacked integrity?
3. Have you exposed yourself to any sexually explicit material?
4. Have you given adequate time to Bible study and prayer?
5. Have you given priority time to your family?
6. Have you fulfilled the mandate of your calling?
7. Have you just lied to me?

If a partner lies about any one of the first six questions, he will have to lie a second time when asked about the seventh one.

Earlier in the book we talked about Bamboo trees and how quickly they seem to shoot up. Their extensive root system requires several years to form beneath the soil, but it is necessary to sustain their tremendous height. The Redwood Trees of California offer us another important analogy. These giant trees grow ninety feet tall, but their root system is only six feet deep. How can such a shallow root system support these enormous trees? The secret is that Redwoods network. They grow in clusters and their root systems join together to strengthen each other. There truly is strength in numbers! This is especially true for believers. We need other Christians. There are no Lone Rangers in the Body of Christ, but if you think about it, even the Lone Ranger had Tonto. Again, I encourage you to establish an accountability relationship if you haven't already.

R stands for *Reliability/Trustworthiness.* Are you reliable? Can people depend on you? Is your word good? When you say something, do you mean it? Do people respect you? Are you able to keep a secret, or are you one of those people who has the reputation that if you are told a secret, it will be all over the church before sundown?

There is a great need for more reliable, solid, steady men and women in the Church today. It is hard to imagine now, but there was a time in America when there was little need for written, legal contracts because a person's word could always be trusted. In some states a handshake is still considered a legally binding agreement. This should still be true for Christians.

Over the years, I have had several Christian businessmen confess to me that if they receive a business card with a Christian symbol on it, they throw it in the trash. It is because they have been burned by other Christians. Sad to say, some Christian are not trustworthy to pay on time either. It grieves my heart to hear that. It is terrible that Christians do these things to one another, but think of the witness this is to the world! Christians should be the most dependable people of all! Our lives should be a fragrant aroma to the world. Just as we can trust the Lord's Word, others should be able to trust ours.

Parents, do your children trust your word? Or do you make promises that you do not keep? Have you promised to take them places and do things for them then not followed through? This might be a small thing in your eyes, but it is magnified in the eyes of a child. This is important for mothers, but even more so with fathers. It is a fact that most young people receive their view of God through their dads. If their earthly fathers are not trustworthy or reliable, how do you think they will view the heavenly Father? Your word has eternal repercussions in the lives of your children.

P stands for *People Person*. As we have discussed throughout this book, secure Christians simply love people. If you truly have the love of Christ in your heart, then His love will flow freely through you to the world around you.

Compassion will propel the gifts of God to flow through you to bring life and healing to the world.

Now, every time you see an advertisement for AARP, let is serve as a reminder to maintain all four of these qualities of a secure Christian leader. After all, you are the best advertisement for God's eternal retirement plan.

Don't Give Up!

Barnabas, like the rest of us, was not perfect, but he humbly allowed the Lord to correct him whenever he needed it. Through the years, I have witnessed many who possessed great potential but who gave up after they failed. Their hearts were not securely grounded enough to continue. Their identity was placed in something other than the Lord; and when they failed, they sunk into depression and self-pity. Totally focused on themselves rather than looking to God for help, they continued on a downward spiral and simply quit.

Also among those whom I have seen give up are those who allowed offenses to grow into bitterness. Once bitterness takes root in a person's life, spiritual vitality is drained and replaced with hatred and many times depression. Then, like a cancer, it spreads to corrupt others. (Hebrews 12:15).

Determine today that regardless of what happens in your life, you are never going to give up. Set your face with unyielding determination that you are not going to quit until you have finished your race. Have the same resolve as great athletes who refuse to give up until they have perfected their respective skills. If someone is willing to do this for a perishable trophy, how much more should we do it for that which is imperishable?

Decide now to be a *champion for Jesus!* He is the undisputed Champion of the Universe! He won that title when He died on the cross and rose again three days later victorious over all of His enemies—sin, sickness, and death! "Where, O death, is your victory? Where, O death, is your sting?" (1 Cor. 15:55). Since you live for the Champion and are on the winning team, go ahead and live like one!

Lord, I am determined to be a champion for Jesus. When I fail or make mistakes, help me to repent quickly, get back on my feet, and persevere till I reach the goal of my calling in Christ. Teach me to both give and receive correction in a manner that reflects Your love, and make me a leader You can be proud of. Amen.

CHAPTER 13

Give 'em a Second Chance!

WE SAW IN THE LAST CHAPTER that that one thing that made Barnabas a champion for Christ was that he refused to quit when he failed. We did not say much about Peter, other than he was the one Paul confronted publicly, but he obviously received Paul's correction and recovered from the failure as well. The fact that he went on to write two epistles that the Holy Spirit chose to become part of the New Testament proves that.

Perhaps one reason that Peter recovered so well was that he had had practice—his two-facedness regarding the Gentiles was not his first major failure. Remember when he denied Jesus? Imagine trying to recover from that! I think that the most wonderful thing about that story, however, is the way in which Jesus restored Peter; and that is the focus of this chapter. A secure believer is one who desires to restore the fallen and does it with the heart that Jesus displayed when He forgave and reinstated Peter in the ministry.

Have you ever really blown it and said something that you wished you could take back? Have you ever been stricken with the all too common "Foot *in* Mouth Disease" rather than the dreaded "Foot and Mouth Disease"? The most tragic part is that when we fall prey to it, it is usually to those who are closest to us, those whom we love the most. If you are like me, you wonder why in the world you ever said some of the things that you have.

Peter could relate, never more so than when he denied Jesus, the One whom he loved the most. To make matters worse, he not only did it once, but *three* times. What anguish and guilt he must have felt when he realized what he had done. I imagine he even wondered if he had somehow committed the unpardonable sin. *Can the Lord ever forgive me and use me again?*

Through this ordeal, Jesus taught Peter what I believe to be one of the most valuable lessons for believers. It is the lesson of humility, which is likely the most difficult subject to master in the school of discipleship for Christians. In my opinion, however, the humility lesson is a most important step in reaching championship status in the Kingdom of God.

So What Is Humility?

Remember, to become a champion, you must resolve never to quit even in the face of adversity, defeat, or opposition. No matter how many times you fall, you must get up and keep pressing on toward the mark that Jesus has placed in front of you.

A true champion is also humble. Let me give you my definition of *humility.* It is simply understanding where your power comes from—it comes from the Lord! Our victories are not due to our own greatness. Any success we have enjoyed has come because the Greater One lives in us! To be humble, then, means that we understand that all of our abilities, talents, intellect, and wit come from Him. As long as we remember that, God can use us! And we all have good motivation to stay in remembrance, because "pride goes before destruction, a haughty spirit before a fall" (Proverbs 16:18)!

With that in mind, there is a common misconception about humility that I want to clear up—humility is not weakness! No! Think about it: if the same power that raised Jesus from the dead lives in you—and it does, if you have made Him Savior and Lord—you could never be considered weak. Why? Because the most powerful force in the universe lives in you! It makes you *strong* in the Lord and the power of His might! Weakness and His power cannot coexist.

So what does this have to do with Peter? Based on his behavior, he had a great deal to learn about humility. If you will recall, he announced several times that he would *never* forsake the Lord even if the other disciples did. Not him! No! Never! But what happened by the time the rooster crowed twice? Peter had denied Jesus three times and in the same evening that he had boasted that he never would! (See Matt. 26:33–35; 69–75.) Pride caused him to fall.

Dejected and wounded, Peter returned to the only thing he knew how to do—fishing. He had not yet learned the lesson of becoming a champion. He had failed, so he quit and went home. This sad pattern is too often repeated among young and immature believers. If immature believers fail, or God does not seem to be answering their prayers, or someone in the church looks at them the wrong way, or the pastor does not acknowledge them, they simply quit church and check out on God. Like Peter, those who give up have not yet learned the lesson of becoming a champion.

But Peter's story did not end there …

Jesus Knew Just How to Handle It

You remember that after Peter denied his Lord, the crucifixion took place. One morning a short time later, Peter came dragging in from a long night of unsuccessful fishing. Imagine the shock when he saw the risen Jesus waiting on the shore with breakfast! As soon as he realized it was Jesus,

Give 'em a Second Chance!

Peter leaped over the side of the boat to meet Him. This is where we pick up our story.

> When they had finished eating, Jesus said to Simon Peter, "Simon son of John, do you truly love me more than these?"
>
> "Yes, Lord," he said, "you know that I love you."
>
> Jesus said, "Feed my lambs."
>
> Again Jesus said, "Simon son of John, do you truly love me?"
>
> He answered, "Yes, Lord, you know that I love you."
>
> Jesus said, "Take care of my sheep."
>
> The third time he said to him, "Simon son of John, do you love me?"
>
> Peter was hurt because Jesus asked him the third time, "Do you love me?" He said, "Lord, you know all things; you know that I love you."
>
> Jesus said, "Feed my sheep."
>
> John 21:15–17

Have you ever asked yourself why Jesus repeated this three times? I have, and I think I know the reason. How many times did Peter deny Jesus? Three times! How many times did Jesus state Peter's call in this passage? Three times! What was Jesus trying to say to Peter? It appears to me that He was saying something like, "I know you blew it. Yes, you let Me down, but Peter, I love you and still desire to use you. I am willing to take a risk on you. Regardless of what you have done, you are still useful to Me."

Can you imagine the impact this had on Peter? This was huge! Sadly today, however, there are very few leaders who would have even considered this kind of restoration. In fact, most would have thrown Peter aside like one throws a disposable bottle in the trash. They probably would have reasoned to themselves that they could find at least ten other people to replace him.

But people are not indispensable! Each person—even if he or she fails—is valuable to the Lord. Jesus could have replaced Peter with the disciple's brother Andrew if He had wanted to, but He did not. Why? In the same way that Barnabas saw past Mark's failure and envisioned what he could become, Jesus saw Peter's potential and was willing to work with him to bring that potential out. Perhaps what took place between Jesus and Peter was the very thing that influenced Barnabas to give Mark a second chance.

The Main Issue

When I played high school football, I remember becoming frustrated with my coaches because they would always yell at me when I did something wrong, but they rarely ever taught me how to do it right. I was well aware of it when I made a mistake such as throwing an interception or missing a block. That was obvious, but in my mind, the mistake itself was not the main issue. The chief point was how to do

it correctly the next time. I was eager to learn, but the coaches were not willing to teach. They preferred to yell.

Since then I have witnessed this same type of behavior countless times in other areas of life. As a youth pastor, I saw parents yell at their children when they did wrong, but they would not take the time to sit down and patiently explain to the child how to do the thing right. I have also witnessed employers and pastors do the same. Authority figures sometimes fail to realize the tremendous power they have in a child or subordinate's life. Their anger, impatience, and intolerance can cause lasting scars Thankfully Jesus does not treat us that way. Although He never winks at sin, He will lovingly teach us the right path to take, if we will stop and listen.

Name Change

What was Peter's call from the Lord? According to our text, he was to shepherd the flock of God's people. Look at verse 15 once again.

> When they had finished eating, Jesus said to Simon Peter, "Simon son of John, do you truly love me more than these?"

Jesus asked Peter if he loved Him more than the others. That may have been a reference to Peter's previous arrogant declaration that he would never desert the Lord even if it meant death. "The other disciples might flee, but not I!" he boasted. (Matt. 26:33.) Jesus gently dealt with the root issue in Peter's life—*pride*. In order for Peter to become an effective leader, it was imperative that he develop a spirit of humility. It is nearly impossible to be a quality Christian leader without it.

It is also next to impossible to develop humility if your identity is in anything other than Jesus. Remember what we talked about earlier: your life is now hidden with Christ in God. (Col. 3:3). You need to die to yourself in order to come alive in Christ Jesus.

Notice something else in verse 15. What did Jesus call him? "Simon." But hadn't Jesus changed his name to "Peter" awhile back? Yes, He had, but "Simon" is the name Jesus used when He first called him to become a *fisher of men.* In effect, what Jesus was saying here was, "Let's start over again with a clean slate."

The name *Peter* means "a rock," and *Simon* means "a reed" that blows in the wind in the shallow parts of a lake. At this point, Peter was not a rock, but rather a reed, tossed to and fro in the breeze. He was impetuous and usually spoke without first considering the ramifications of what he was about to say. Jesus, however, could see through it all and believed that Peter could develop into the *rock* that he needed to become. He believed this so strongly that He even changed his name. I am sure that the other disciples snickered when Jesus first called Peter a rock! At that time, he was anything but one! But, every time Jesus called his name,

Give 'em a Second Chance!

He spoke a faith-filled word about Peter's destiny. "Hey, *Rock*, come over here!" Jesus kept speaking it until it became a reality in Peter's life. It doesn't matter what others have said about you, listen only to what God says and keep speaking that until it becomes a reality in your life!

But, how does one become a *rock?* It is a paradox: if you want to become a rock—solid and steady—you must first learn *humility.* If you want to go up, you must first go down. It is that same Kingdom thinking that we talked about earlier in the book. So often it is the opposite of the world's way.

If, on the other hand, you want to be in control of your own life rather than giving Jesus the reigns, then you will become an unstable blade of grass blowing in the wind. You will not be trustworthy or reliable enough for the Lord to use you. Again Solomon said it aptly:

Pride ends in humiliation,
while humility brings honor.

Proverbs 29:23 NLT

Because Jesus believed in Peter, an amazing transformation took place shortly after the encounter in John 21. Acts 2 recounts that Peter was filled with the Holy Spirit on the Day of Pentecost and began to preach boldly. As a result, around three thousand people were baptized and added to the church! (vv. 1–4, 14–41.) And he was just getting started. In the face of great persecution and much opposition, Peter never gave up but continued preaching and winning countless people for the Lord, healing the sick, and raising the dead. He was even the first person to take the Gospel to the Gentiles. Think what the early Church would have missed had Jesus given up on Peter!

This is a wonderful truth that we must never forget! I thank God regularly for never giving up on me when I have made mistakes. God always sees our potential. He sees what you can become if you will not give up but will allow Him to continually work in your life.

Peter's Commitment

> Jesus said, "… I tell you the truth, when you were younger you dressed yourself and went where you wanted; but when you are old you will stretch out your hands, and someone else will dress you and lead you where you do not want to go." Jesus said this to indicate the kind of death by which Peter would glorify God. Then he said to him, "Follow me!"
>
> John 21:18–19

In verse 18, Jesus used a Hebrew proverbial statement describing old age to prophecy that Peter was going to die by crucifixion in the years to come. If you think about it, this must have been a startling revelation. Peter now understood that if he continued to follow Jesus' call for the rest of his

life, he would die a martyr's death by crucifixion! Think about the implications of that for a few moments.

Now, let's bring it closer to home. What about you? What if you knew that in continuing to follow Jesus' plan for your life, you, too, would die a martyr's death? Would you still obey His calling? Peter did! He truly became the unshakeable rock that his name indicated he would become.

The Point of No Return

Many year ago when Lisa and I first became involved in overseas missions, I had a special encounter with the Lord in Brownsville, Texas. We were with a team of people preparing to go into Matamoras, Mexico, for a day of street evangelism. Before we left, I pulled away from the rest of the group to spend a few moments in the Word with the Lord. As I read the two verses above, it was as if time was suspended for a split second. The events of my life flashed before my eyes, and in my heart I sensed the Lord asking me, *If you knew right now that you were going to die a martyr's death for serving Me, would you still do it?*

It was an awesome moment of decision for me. How sincere and deep was my commitment to the Lord? I cannot express in mere words what that moment was like. Many give lip service, but this required much more. I did not quickly answer because I understood the gravity of the question. I knew I had to be totally honest with myself and with Him. But in only a few minutes, a deep conviction rose up inside me and I declared boldly, "Yes, Lord, I would still obey you, even if I knew it would mean martyrdom!" I sensed Him smiling at my statement.

Now, He did not say I *would* die a martyr's death; He just asked if I was willing. As the One who knows what is in our hearts, He already knew the answer. Why, then, did He ask it? To reveal to me what was in my own heart. It was a point of decision, a line of demarcation, for me. I had to come to the place where I knew there was no going back. I had reached the point of no return!

Charles Lindbergh, the first to safely cross the Atlantic Ocean in an airplane, reached a point in his journey that pilots call *the point of no return*. It was the place where it would have taken more fuel to return to North America than it would to continue on to Europe. Once he reached that spot, he would either succeed or die.

Have you reached the point of no return in your life journey? It is a place to which all who are consistently used by the Lord must arrive. You have to purpose in your heart that regardless of how many times you fail, what others do or do not do, you are going to keep serving Him. Hopefully I can speak for you too, but I have determined that even if the most respected leaders in the Body of Christ fall into sin, I am going to keep following Jesus. People I have great confidence in may fail me or try to abuse me, but I will never deny nor forsake my Lord. Those who can say these things and really mean them are true champions in the making.

If you have not yet arrived at this juncture in your walk with the Lord, I encourage you to take a few moments right now to talk to Him about this. Purpose in your heart that—regardless of what happens—you will never deny Him or walk away from His plan for your life. I promise, you will never regret it!

Control Freaks

So many people are afraid to come to this place because they do not trust that the Lord will do what is best for them. Oh, they say that God is good and they know He loves them. But in reality they fear that He will ask them to live in a grass hut in a steamy, malaria-infested jungle somewhere overseas. Those who use that excuse do not really know the true nature of God, for He first gives the desire for the thing He wills, then He supplies the gifts needed to accomplish it. The feelings, however, usually follow the willingness to obey. We take the first step, and God does the rest.

If you think about it, the real issue with this step is control. Who is actually in control of your life? You or God? It requires humility to release your life, your future, and your all to the Lord. From one who has taken that step, I can assure you that you will never regret doing so. I believe

Peter, Barnabas, Paul, and every other believer in history who has made an impact on this world has taken that step.

I am not telling you something that I have not had to walk through myself. For nearly twenty-five years, I believed God to heal my eyes and ears, but they only grew worse. It was a real test of faith, but I decided that the only option I had was to keep going to the nations to fulfill His call on my life. It has sure been better than sitting at home and feeling sorry for myself.

"Follow Me!"

Returning to our narrative between Jesus and Peter, let's again look at John 21:19. "Then [Jesus] said to him, 'Follow me!'" At that moment, Jesus restored Peter and reinstated him in the ministry. All the failures and all the denials did not matter now. Jesus' call had not changed. In fact, "God's gifts and his call can never be withdrawn" (Rom. 11:29 NLT). I find it interesting that Jesus chose to use the very same words—"Follow me!"—that He had used three years earlier when He initially called Peter along those very same shores. (Matt. 4:19.) Imagine how they must have comforted and strengthened Peter throughout the remainder of his life of faithful service.

In the original Greek text, the tense used is present imperative, meaning that John 21:19 literally means,

Give 'em a Second Chance!

"Keep following Me!" Jesus was saying to Peter, "Regardless of what you encounter in your life and the obstacles that you will have to overcome, keep following Me. Keep preaching and tending the flock I have called you to watch over. No matter what happens, stay on the course I have laid out for you."

The focus for Peter, then, was not to be on circumstances or even what would happen in the future. What was really going to matter was whether or not he was faithfully following the Lord at any given moment. The same is true for you. Your focus should not be so much on where you are headed but whether you are obeying the Lord right now, today. This is not to minimize the goal, but in order to reach it, you must live in God's will now and at every moment until you get there. That is not to say that you will never miss it, but as soon as you realize that you have, repent and get back on course. Like Peter, you can always begin again.

At the end of your days when you stand before the Lord, He will ask you one question. It will not be a doctrinal question, nor will it be a question concerning someone else's life. It will simply be: "Were you obedient to My call on your life?"—nothing more and nothing less.

So … how do you answer that question right now?

I believe Jesus was continuing to make this point as His conversation with Peter progressed:

> Peter turned and saw that the disciple whom Jesus loved was following them. (This was the one who had leaned back against Jesus at the supper and had said, "Lord, who is going to betray you?") When Peter saw him, he asked, "Lord, what about him?"
>
> Jesus answered, "If I want him to remain alive until I return, what is that to you? You must follow me." Because of this, the rumor spread among the brothers that this disciple would not die. But Jesus did not say that he would not die; he only said, "If I want him to remain alive until I return, what is that to you?"
>
> John 21:20–23

This scene is so typically human. If the subject weren't so serious, it would be comical. Here Peter had just been told that he would die a martyr's death, and what was he concerned about? He wanted to know what John's fate was going to be. Jesus, of course, could see through this and said that if He wanted John to remain alive until He returned that was none of his concern. The only thing that Peter needed to be concerned about was whether or not he was obedient to Jesus. In the same way, we are not responsible for the call on anyone's life but our own.

Evidently, Peter was thinking that if he was going to have to die as a martyr, he did not want to do it by himself. But as I stated before, when the day comes for you to stand before the Lord, you will stand there alone. Each of us will stand before Him individually, separately, giving account for our own personal lives.

Give 'em a Second Chance!

The Comparison Game

One of the inherent dangers of living a life of insecurity is that the insecure person will compare him- or herself to others. This is a hazardous game, although those whose identity is not in Jesus play it often. This was exactly what Peter was doing as he attempted to compare his destiny with that of John. The same game is played today. In fact you have probably witnessed it many times:

Insecure mothers may compare their children with other kids, or they may feel like lesser women if they are not able to bear children like their friends.

Insecure women may compare their dress size with that of a friend who wears four sizes smaller. Because they are no longer able to fit into the clothes they wore in college, they may feel less secure.

Insecure men may compare their jobs with those of their friends. They may base their personal self-worth on how much money they make or the value that society places on their particular occupation.

Insecure pastors may compare the size of their congregation with that of a larger church across town and feel inadequate. They may also be insecure about their lack of eloquence and compare their delivery style to that of other pastors they know.

THE *Barnabas* FACTOR

The problem with playing the comparison game is that it leads to other vices, such as jealousy, envy, criticizing, and gossip. Although it is not impossible to break free from this trap, once a person falls into it, it is very difficult. Again, Solomon had keen insight:

> Anger is cruel and fury overwhelming,
> but who can stand before jealousy?
>
> Proverbs 27:4

Couple jealousy with self-pity (which is actually a form of pride), and you have a tremendously volatile combination. One of the worst things about this problem is that these attitudes are highly contagious. It is especially damaging when they are passed down to the children in a family. Unless the cycle is broken, these negative emotions and behaviors will likely grow stronger with each successive generation.

I have seen an example of this in Central America. A pastor I know there built an incredibly large church in less than five years. In fact, the building is as nice as any church in the United States. It has all of latest technology and like many churches in Latin America it also has incredible worship. But instead of celebrating this pastor's success, many of the other pastors in his city have chosen to criticize him for various reasons. As far as they are concerned, nothing he does is right.

Isn't it sad that instead of rejoicing that the Kingdom of God is expanding in their city, they are jealous that it has seemingly been so easy for him. I want to stand up and yell, "Hey, we are all on the same team! Instead of fighting each other, why not work together?"

If, on the other hand, a pastor's identity is in Christ and not in the size of his ministry, he is free to rejoice when a brother's church grows and prospers. If it brings joy to the Lord, it should bless our hearts as well.

The same is true in business and in every arena of life. If your brother or sister is prospering more than you are, why not rejoice instead of becoming jealous? God is no respecter of persons. If you will keep your heart right and put your faith in Him, He will prosper you too. But this is a conscious decision that we each have to make. Just like the firm resolve necessary for us to overcome offenses and bitterness, we must choose not to allow jealousy to enter our thoughts. If it does, we must take it captive along with every thought that raises its ugly head in opposition to the knowledge of God! (2 Cor. 10:5.) We need to see jealousy as the devilish monster that it really is, for we cannot afford to entertain it and its malevolent cousins that will certainly follow.

The Rock

Church tradition tells us that at the end of his life, Peter was led to the place of crucifixion by his wife. She wept that her husband was about to be executed and die a hideous death. Peter, however, did not lament but rather rejoiced. He, in fact, exhorted his wife to remain strong in the Lord and to remember the example that the Lord Jesus Christ had set when He went to the cross. To Peter, the least that he could do was die for Him.

Who was that? *Simon, the reed,* or *Peter, the rock?* Peter, now, was as solid as a rock. The man no longer existed who had denied Jesus three times and joined his fellow disciples in flight when the Lord was arrested. Further, he was no longer the boasting, impetuous fisherman he had been when Jesus called him. Peter had become steadfast and immovable yet also humble. He had become the man Jesus proclaimed that he would become—the rock!

Peter's pending execution came as no surprise to him. He never forgot what Jesus had predicted concerning his death. In fact, in his last letter he wrote: "I know that I will soon put [my body] aside, as our Lord Jesus Christ has made clear to me" (2 Peter 1:14). He had known this day would come, yet he did not shrink back from his call. He was faithful to the Lord's words, "Follow Me!" and remained obedient to the heavenly vision and God's dream for his life.

Let Him Transform You

If God was able to transform Peter so completely, think what He can do for you! No matter what you are like today or

what you have done in the past, the Lord can mold you into a productive servant. He is not only able to do it, He earnestly desires to. He is the God of redemption; He is the God of restoration; and He is the God of transformation. It is His nature. Jesus is always willing to restore and to reinstate us.

One common mistake that believers make is not allowing the Lord to change them because they simply cannot forgive themselves. Consequently they slip into self-pity and depression. Self-pity paralyzes spiritual growth and even causes a person to digress spiritually. If you think about it, not being able to forgive ourselves when the Lord is willing to forgive us is really a form of pride. We should avoid self-pity and discouragement like the plague and recognize that they are sins as serious as lust or stealing. We must do this if we are intent on achieving championship status in the Kingdom of God.

If you have failed and are in need of restoration, begin to pray for God to bring a Barnabas into your life. It is much easier to walk through the steps of restoration with a trusted, mature believer by your side. Even then, remember that Jesus is the Friend who sticks closer than a brother. (Prov. 18:24.)

Flexible Rocks?

When architects build skyscrapers, they design flexibility into the structure for strength. If you have ever been to the top of one, you know that you can actually feel the building sway slightly in the wind. Many malls in the United States are designed with this kind of flexibility as well. When the mall is full of people, you can often feel the floors bounce ever so slightly. It is rather unnerving when you first notice it.

The beauty of this design is that when the ground shakes, as in an earthquake for example, flexible structures give, then return to their original position. Rigid buildings, on the other hand, crumble. The flexible structures are simply much stronger and can take much more punishment than rigid ones.

Similarly, God created trees with some of the same attributes. One of the main purposes of a tree's root system is to anchor it securely in place. Healthy trees, even very large and tall ones, can withstand incredibly strong wind storms when the root system has developed properly and been well nourished. If ever you do see a tree uprooted as a result of a storm, it is generally due to some type of failure in the root system, which can be caused by any number of things. This points again to how critical it is for us to nourish our spiritual roots in Christ and His Word.

With these things in mind, could I possibly describe Simon Peter as the *flexible rock?* (Simon the flexible reed plus Peter the rock.) Actually, I believe God desires for all believers to be *flexible rocks.* We are to be well grounded, not easily moved like a rock, while at the same time we

must remain bendable enough for the Lord to direct our course wherever He desires. We never outgrow the need to be flexible, and since there is a tendency to become rigid as we age, we must guard against it more with each passing year. It is common for a believer to have developed humility as a young person only to lose it later in life to pride masked by religiosity. Paul described this kind of person as "having a form of godliness but denying its power" (2 Tim. 3:5).

The reason we must avoid becoming rigid and religious is that both are rooted in pride. They indicate that a person is not spending time in the life-changing presence of the Lord on a daily basis. Think about it. How could anyone be arrogant in the company of the Lord? Those who walk humbly before Him are the ones who are flexible and open to new directives from Him, no matter how uncomfortable they seem. The wise understand that change is an inevitable part of life. The more we are able to go with the flow of God's Spirit, the more fruitful our lives will be and the more we will enjoy the ride.

Thankfully, the Lord in His mercy will place signs along the way to get our attention, like the ones that say, "Caution! Wet Floor!" Through the Holy Spirit, He will warn you of this impending hazard. The trick is to heed His warnings instead of becoming so oblivious to His presence that we kick the signs out of the way without first reading them.

THE *B*ARNABAS FACTOR

Putting on the *cloak of humility* is our best protection. In the next chapter we will examine how to do this.

> *Lord, thank You for never giving up on me. When I fall, help me to forgive myself and get back on track. Help me to recognize when any fruit of insecurity raises its ugly head. I refuse to play the comparison game, but I rejoice with those who rejoice and look to You as my source of blessing. Help me to be solid as a rock yet flexible in Your hand. No matter what, I will remain faithful to you and fulfill the call You have placed on my life. Amen.*

CHAPTER 14

The Cloak of Humility

THROUGHOUT THIS BOOK, we have discussed the importance of believers finding their personal security in Christ, that is, believers who have incorporated the *Barnabas Factor* into their lives. Nowhere is the need greater than in Christian leaders today. In fact, the problem is so pervasive that I believe it has actually hindered the spread of the Gospel. It makes sense, however. If the enemy can keep the leaders in the Body of Christ bound up with personal fears and insecurities, then the flocks under them will never be able to reach out to the world with the liberating message of Jesus Christ. Insecure leaders are generally inward in their focus; consequently, most of their followers are as well.

Sad to say, these insecure leaders never obtain championship status in the Kingdom. They are missing the all-important key that unlocks the entrance to that lofty level. What is the key? *Humility*, and few ever obtain it. *Humility* is solid evidence that the *Barnabas Factor* is at work in a believer's life, for it is impossible to be truly humble if a person is not secure in who he or she is in Christ. I can only surmise that Barnabas was an extremely humble man, or he would not have been able to quietly accomplish all that he did for the Lord.

In the last chapter we talked about the importance of humility and how it was a critical lesson that Peter learned in his walk with the Lord. Who, then, would have more authority than he to address other leaders about this critical issue after his many years of faithful service? I do not think it is any coincidence that God chose him for this task. The following passage clearly reveals the incredible transformation that had taken place in his life. They are words of advice for the ages, and they have never been more necessary than today.

> To the elders among you, I appeal as a fellow elder, a witness of Christ's sufferings and one who also will share in the glory to be revealed: Be shepherds of God's flock that is under your care, serving as overseers—not because you must, but because you are willing, as God wants you to be; not greedy for money, but eager to serve; not lording it over those entrusted to you, but being examples to the flock.

The Cloak of Humility

And when the Chief Shepherd appears, you will receive the crown of glory that will never fade away.

Young men, in the same way be submissive to those who are older. All of you, clothe yourselves with humility toward one another, because,

"God opposes the proud

but gives grace to the humble."

Humble yourselves, therefore, under God's mighty hand, that he may lift you up in due time.

1 Peter 5:1–6

Before I break down these verses, let me explain the context. In 1 Peter 4, Peter taught that judgment begins with "the house of God" (v.17 KJV). Our text from chapter 5 is a continuation of that theme. Peter's line of reasoning goes something like this: If judgment begins with the Church, it must first come to the leaders of the Church who ultimately influence the direction of the Church. Although this passage can be applied to all believers, it is specifically addressed to "the elders." Leaders carry greater responsibility and thus must be exemplary representatives of Christ in all they do.

As we stated in the beginning of this book, nearly everyone is in some position of leadership. Whether it is in the home, school, work, or church, most believers are leaders; thus these words of Peter are pertinent to each of us. There is one area in which every believer is definitely a leader and that is as we lead by example the unbelieving world.

The first thing I notice when I read this passage is a real spirit of humility in Peter. Noticeably absent is his previous boastful arrogance. No longer trusting in his own ability, he now understood that God was the Source for all that he had and did, that any ability, talent, or success he enjoyed could be attributed to Him alone. This attitude is diametrically opposed to the spirit of this age, the secular humanism that applauds self-assertion and self-promotion.

When we consider the following verse, we understand just how important developing humility is:

> To fear the Lord is to hate evil;
> > I hate pride and arrogance,
> > evil behavior and perverse speech.
>
> Proverbs 8:13

Quite simply, God *hates* pride and arrogance.

Why? For starters, it was the sin that led to Lucifer's (Satan's) rebellion and subsequent banishment from heaven. In us, it shows a lack of appreciation for what the Lord has done for us. To believe the lie that everything we possess and all of our achievements are the direct result of our own merit is the height of arrogance; it is ludicrous. Yet, most of us have to continually battle thoughts of pride.

An example from my own life is when I have preached a message at a church and those who have been blessed by it tell me so. On the drive home, the devil may plant a thought like, *I am pretty good. Yes, I am a good preacher!* If I dwell on that, pride could begin to take root. Pride then leads to arrogance. The thing about pride and arrogance is that they are so subtle. If we are not actively on alert looking for them, they may go undetected.

Solomon understood the danger that accompanies praise and issued the following warning:

> The crucible for silver and the furnace for gold,
> but man is tested by the praise he receives.
>
> Proverbs 27:21

Why is a person tested by praise? Praise reveals whether a person is truly humble or not. Whatever is in a person's heart will manifest itself—not only in times of hardship but also in moments of praise. If your identity is rooted in Jesus, you will have no trouble deflecting the praise to the Lord. An insecure person, on the other hand, will likely feed on the praise of others.

When people pat me on the back, I thank them verbally, but inwardly I make a conscious effort to thank the Lord for His grace, which enabled me to do what He has called me to do. I know that all the good in my life has come from Him. I shudder to think what and where I would be without His love and mercy.

Many people tell Lisa and me how great it is that we are willing to travel to dangerous locations and stay in less than desirable places all over the world. This may surprise you, but in all honesty we love it! God has given us the grace and the desire to do what He has called us to do, but we are no more commendable than anyone else in the Body of Christ. We are only doing what He requires of us. He may ask others to stay home and make money to support His work around the world. If it weren't for them, missionaries like us could not fulfill our calling. In the eyes of the Lord, we are all equally important parts of the process.

The Common Denominator

I heard a pastor make an astute observation concerning arrogance, and it is worth repeating here. When asked in an interview what are the signs that a Christian leader is going to fall into adultery or some other sin, he stated that he could think of several people who had fallen. The only common denominator he observed was that shortly before these ministers fell, he noticed each one had become arrogant. This should come as no surprise because Scripture predicts this: "Pride goes before destruction, a haughty spirit before a fall" (Prov. 16:18).

If you think about it, this makes sense. When a leader begins to operate in pride and arrogance, he is no longer trusting the Lord or operating in the fear of the Lord. This is an extremely dangerous place to be. It is like standing on thin ice, which will break unless the person steps off of it. The person who stays in pride is outside God's protective

The Cloak of Humility

covering and becomes open game for the devil's temptation. Without a humble spirit that is in vital communion with the Lord, a fall is sure to follow. That is why God hates it so. We should hate it as well.

When pride and lust are combined in an individual, they create a highly combustible vulnerability in the person's character. Lust says, "I need it now!" Then pride joins in, arrogantly boasting, "I deserve it for all I do for the Lord!" Then the ugly cousin *deception* moves in and reasons, "I'm sure God will just wink at this." By the time these have joined forces, the leader is ready to explode. A tiny spark is all that is needed to ignite this highly flammable combination, a catalyst that the enemy is all too happy to provide.

Having established how these evil cousins operate and understanding how much God hates them, we can safely conclude that God absolutely delights in the antithesis—humility. This delectable fruit is one we all should strive to cultivate in our lives. This is an area in which an accountability partner can be a priceless gift. Because of the subtlety of pride, it is easy to become blinded by its affects. An astute accountability partner can help you recognize pride when it begins lurking around you. A good spouse is a real asset in this area as well, more to be cherished than gold and silver—I know from experience!

Humility Does Not Pull Rank

Now, let's look at several specific comments that Peter made in his first epistle concerning humility.

> To the elders among you, I appeal as a fellow elder, a witness of Christ's sufferings and one who also will share in the glory to be revealed.
>
> 1 Peter 5:1

Did you catch Peter's heart in this first verse? Think about it: he was not only one of the original twelve disciples, but he was also a part of the inner three (Peter, James, and John) of Jesus' most trusted friends. If anyone had the right to pull rank, it was Peter. An insecure leader certainly would have, but not this godly leader. He did not think more highly of himself than he should have. Sometimes leaders are too impressed with themselves and use their positions to throw their weight around. Peter, on the other hand, humbly appealed to the other leaders as his equals. Notice the inclusive language, calling the leaders "fellow elders." I surmise, however, that the other leaders did not consider themselves his peers. They no doubt had great respect and admiration for him, but because of humility, he dared not take advantage of it.

In like manner, in the book of Philemon, Paul took this same approach in dealing with the letter's namesake over his runaway slave, Onesimus. Evidently, Paul had led Philemon

to the Lord and enjoyed a close relationship with him. Later, while Paul was imprisoned in Rome, Onesimus escaped and made his way to that city where he met up with Paul and become a believer himself.

Now, Paul, desiring to make the situation right, wrote to Philemon on behalf of Onesimus, asking for forgiveness. Legally, at that time in history, Philemon could have had Onesimus put to death! Yet Paul wrote, "Although in Christ I could be bold and order you to do what you ought to do, yet I appeal to you on the basis of love" (Philem. vv. 8–9). Even though Paul had apostolic authority over Philemon, he did not assert it. Instead he humbly appealed to him as a friend to forgive Onesimus of his crime. Evidently, Philemon followed Paul's urging because the account is part of the New Testament we enjoy today.

Finally, if there ever was someone who could have thrown his weight around, it was James, the author of the book that bears his name. In addition to being the top leader of the Jerusalem church, he was also the half-brother of Jesus! But notice how he introduced himself: "This letter is from James, a slave of God and of the Lord Jesus Christ" (James 1:1 NLT). While he certainly had the right to broadcast his credentials, he chose to characterize himself as a slave of God and the Lord Jesus! He understood that it was in Him that his value lay, not in a title or because he was related by natural birth to Jesus. This humility was the basis of his authority, not his so-called qualifications.

No wonder the early Church grew so rapidly. With so many secure and truly humble leaders like Barnabas, Paul, Peter, and James, the Holy Spirit could have free reign.

Leadership Based on Position

There are two primary ways to lead people. The first is based on *position.* Leaders who lead from this perspective often utter words like: "I am the boss, and you had better submit." Or, they may never actually say it, but the attitude is obvious based on their demeanor. Naturally this is a fruit of insecurity. This style of leadership may work in the short-term—in crisis management, for example—but it will begin to disintegrate over a long period of time.

Cultural considerations come into play at this point. In many cultures around the world, this is the only method of leadership that is ever exhibited. In Western cultures, however, this style breaks down quickly because Westerners typically want their opinions and ideas to be seen and heard. Westerners like to think of themselves as "chiefs" (or leaders) rather than "Indians" (or followers).

I have witnessed missions teams break up over this very issue. It usually happens when the person in charge is from a non-Western culture in which leaders are rarely questioned or challenged. When people from the United States or Australia, for example, are placed on the team as subordinates, sparks can fly when they want to add their two cents' worth. What the Westerners fail to understand is that in other cultures, there is a respected gap between leaders and subordinates. Non-Westerners would never think of making suggestions to a leader.

Similarly, if leaders from Western cultures are insecure, they may try to lead from a strong dictatorial position. They, too, are threatened when the other teammates offer their input. Naturally, this undermines the unity and effectiveness of the team.

This type of leadership is not relegated to business or ministry. It often takes place in the home. How many people have said that theirs fathers were aloof men? They may describe these men as hard, demanding, and rather detached. Needless to say, the leadership of men like this is ineffective in their families. How important it is to remember that Jesus, not our culture, is to be our example of leadership.

Leadership Based on Relationship

This is the second and more successful way to lead. Secure leaders understand that they have rank and position over others, but they rarely use either as leverage. They typically reserve that for managing crisis situations. The majority of the time these leaders appeal to their subordinates much like Peter did in his letter to the elders—as a fellow laborer in the Kingdom. These kinds of quality relationships, however, are much harder to cultivate, for they require time, effort, and energy. The investment, however, is well worth it for it yields a level of respect and loyalty that flows from the heart. Instead of subordinates following orders through gritted teeth, they gladly serve the leader. It is amazing what others will do for this type of leader and how effective this style of leadership is. The "secret ingredient" is humility. My dad used to say it to me this way: "Others do not care how much you know until they know how much you care."

This type of leadership is badly needed in homes as well as in ministries and businesses. Dads, do your children know how much you care about them? I am not talking about the fact that you provide a house and clothes for them. Do you show them in ways they can relate to, by your kind words and your loving embraces on a daily basis? And while we are at it, are you communicating your love for your wife in ways that she can appreciate?

Moms, you are naturally more relational, but are your children getting the message that you care deeply for them? If you think about it, many of us lead in our homes the same way we witnessed our own parents do it. The problem with this is that many had parents who were poor examples, although those moms and dads may have done the best they could. Who, then, should be our model? Jesus, of course!

The Cloak of Humility

Words of Wisdom from Peter

> Be shepherds of God's flock that is under your care, serving as overseers—not because you must, but because you are willing, as God wants you to be; not greedy for money, but eager to serve; not lording it over those entrusted to you, but being examples to the flock.
>
> vv. 2–3

There are many aspects of Christian leadership that we could discuss from these two verses, but I want to highlight three points relevant to our present discussion on humility.

First, *the flock belongs to God.* The leader is merely the shepherd or overseer of the people, the one appointed to care for them. When a leader understands this, he or she will be set free from the *possession mentality* that is so prevalent among Christian leadership. Leaders who are insecure are almost always possessive of their people and territory. There is a big difference between caring for the flock and the leader feeling like the sheep belong to him or her. Leaders are not owners. God is the owner; the leaders are merely His hired hands. Likewise in regard to families, parents do not own their children. The heavenly Father merely entrusts children to their parents for a season. When the children reach adulthood, parents are to send them off with their blessing and not try to hold on to them or control them.

Second, *leaders are to be servants, not lords.* As Jesus so eloquently elaborated to His disciples, the world's style of leadership is to lord it over others, but this is not the way of the Kingdom of God. As we have discussed before, the Christian style of leadership is servant leadership, and here Peter exhorts leaders to be eager to serve. This same servant's heart should also pervade leadership in the home.

Third, *leaders are not to be greedy for money.* We must each ask ourselves, *Why am I serving the Lord? What is my true motive?* We are to serve God's people because we love them and desire to obey the Lord's call, not for notoriety or financial gain. Solomon again provided keen insight: "A greedy man stirs up dissension, but he who trusts in the Lord will prosper" (Prov. 28:25). If there is constant strife in your home, church, ministry, or workplace, greed could be the root cause. It brings with it all kinds of evil. To combat greed, leaders are to be generous with their people and not hoard up the blessings for themselves. The same holds true in families as fathers should be generous to both their wives and their children.

An Additional Word Regarding Finances

I do not mean that Lisa or I heard an audible voice, but we believe God told us that if we would build His house, He would build ours. In other words, if we would minister wherever He leads and not make our decisions based on how much money a church is able give to us, He would bless us!

The Cloak of Humility

As we have followed through on our commitment to Him, we have seen God fulfill His part over and over again.

One thing that we have learned is that the size of a church does not necessarily determine the amount of an offering. We have preached in small churches and received large offerings. On the other hand, one time we spoke in a rather large church and had a tremendous service. Over half of the congregation came to the altar to commit themselves to reaching the lost around the world. Despite the success of the meeting, however, that church did not give us any offering at all! This gave us the opportunity to forgive and to remind ourselves that God is our source and not any church.

But guess what happened next? Two weeks after that incident, we preached in another church and received the largest offering we had ever received from a church! I firmly believe it was because Lisa and I kept our hearts pure. The same is true for you—if you keep your heart pure, God will bless you. Pastor Billy Joe Daugherty of Victory Christian Center in Tulsa, Oklahoma, often says, "If you don't get bitter, you will make it in ministry." How true that statement is!

The Lord has repeatedly demonstrated to us that He is our source and not people or churches. He will use people as the channel to bring His blessings to us, but we must always remember that He is the ultimate source.

The Reward

Next, Peter shared what faithful leaders can expect to receive from the Lord.

> When the Chief Shepherd appears, you will receive the crown of glory that will never fade away.
>
> v. 4

For those who obey their calling, walk in humility, maintain the heart of a servant, and make people the aim and not financial gain, Jesus the Chief Shepherd will reward with a crown of glory when He appears. Note that He is referred to here as the Chief Shepherd. This reminds us that Christian leaders are under shepherds who serve the Chief Shepherd. Jesus himself told us that whatever we do for others we are actually doing for Him. (See Matt. 10:42.) He is the Lord!

In today's world, where many leaders are serving for all the wrong reasons, this should be a warning to examine the motives of our hearts and determine if we are truly serving the Lord for the right reasons.

I don't know about you, but I would like to receive a crown of glory from the Lord as a reward for my faithfulness to Him. I seek His affirmation and none other. I have a hunch that in heaven there will be a multitude of saints wearing crowns, most of whom were never famous. In their ranks will be mothers and grandmothers who faithfully prayed for years without any honors afforded to them here on Earth. There will also be little-known missionaries who committed their lives to serve in remote jungles to take the Gospel to people who would have never heard it otherwise. Their work may have been done in obscurity here on Earth, but heaven knows all about it. When the recognition really counts, these are the ones who will hear, "Well done!" from the Lord as He places an incorruptible crown on their heads.

Biblical Submission

Picking up again with Peter's exhortation:

> Young men, in the same way be submissive to those who are older. All of you, clothe yourselves with humility toward one another, because, "God opposes the proud but gives grace to the humble."
>
> v. 5

Notice that first he mentioned *submission.* Submission? It is almost considered a dirty word in today's society. In a world where individualism is venerated, submission to others sounds as strange as having two heads. In fact, when the subject is mentioned in certain circles, the people may look at you like *you* have two heads! For many, the term stirs up images of racism or some form of abuse by authority figures, but neither is included in the biblical definition.

The first step to submitting to another person is to become humble. Notice that Peter told the younger men to submit to the leadership of the older, more experienced men. Instead of seeing the older crowd as out of step with the times, younger men and women should view them with respect and esteem their wisdom and experience as more valuable than all the wealth in the world.

When I first began in the ministry, the Lord spoke to me about this very subject of submission. I was serving in another man's ministry at the time, even though I had a vision for my own ministry and knew the direction I was headed. The Lord revealed a truth to me, which I believe has impacted my life in more ways than I may ever realize here on Earth. He said, *The kind of servant you are in another man's ministry will determine the kind of servants I bring you when you are in your own ministry. Therefore, serve this man in the very way you would want someone else to serve you.*

I knew what He meant. As Peter stated, I was to submit to the elders over me in ministry. I was to *put on the cloak of humility* in order to serve just as Jesus did when He washed the disciples' feet. Perhaps this is the same image that Peter had in mind when he penned the words in his epistle. Jesus literally chose to take on the nature of a servant when He came to the earth. He "made himself nothing, taking the very nature of a servant, being made in human likeness" (Phil. 2:7).

In over twenty years of ministry and having worked with literally thousands of young people, I have rarely witnessed any who have been willing to truly follow Jesus' example of service. Most want instant success. Many tell us that they want to be where we are in ministry, and I remind them that we did not get to our present place overnight. What they see now is a product of years of faithfully submitting and serving, mostly in other people's ministries. There are some things you can only learn through experience, and these are the types of things I learned while helping, assisting, and serving others in ministry. I could fill another book on all the lessons that I have gleaned.

Humility and Grace

Referring again to 1 Peter 5:5, you will notice that the command "to clothe yourselves with humility" was given to all believers. Why? It is the way of the Kingdom, and as the above passage states, God promises that He gives *grace* to the humble. On the other hand, He opposes the proud! When we consider the outcome of Korah in Numbers 16, we realize it is not good to be in opposition to the Lord! "Haughtiness goes before destruction; humility precedes honor" (Prov. 18:12 NLT).

So many Christian teachers speak and write on the subject of grace, but few emphasize that the first step to receiving grace is to become *humble* as Peter taught. A common definition of *grace* is that it is "unmerited favor";

however, God only gives this grace to certain people—the humble! Without humility, you cannot have God's favor.

With that thought in mind, I am concerned about the Church in the United States in particular and all Western countries in general. The fact is, humility is a rare commodity in contemporary Western society. When I travel to non-Western nations and witness the genuine humility in the believers there, the glaring arrogance of the West is made that much more apparent to me. I often wonder, *How much longer will God tolerate our pride before He begins to oppose us and exalt other nations?* This is an area where much prayer is needed. In the United States, our forefathers were humble people. They were utterly dependent on God for their very survival. Over time, however, many in America have taken its success and prosperity for granted, forgetting that it has been blessed because of God's grace.

Daily Confession

For these reasons, it is imperative that we strive for humility. As a part of my own effort to do so, I put on the armor of God every morning and add a twist at the end. I confess, "Lord, I put on the helmet of salvation, the breastplate of righteousness, and I gird my loins with the belt of truth. I put on the shoes for the preparation of the Gospel, and I take up the shield of faith and the sword of the Spirit." (See Eph. 6:11–17.) Then I finish my confession by saying, "I

The Cloak of Humility

put on the cloak of humility!" I take this additional step because pride will render ineffective all of that wonderful armor that the Lord provides.

Humility Yields Promotion

Continuing with Peter's exhortation,

> Humble yourselves, therefore, under God's mighty hand, that he may lift you up in due time.
>
> v. 6

God promises to exalt the humble. That is certainly good news, but notice that this promise is qualified by the phrase "in due time." Promotion will come, but it will be at the right time and at the right place. "Fear of the LORD teaches a person to be wise; humility precedes honor" (Prov. 15:33 NLT 96). The arrogant and the prideful promote themselves and boast about their accomplishments, but the humble allow the Lord to do it. When God exalts, you will be ready for the new responsibility.

In my own life, I often wondered why promotion did not come as quickly as I would have liked. I knew God had called me to have my own ministry and to take His Word to the nations, but things did not open up as quickly as I would have liked. I used to repeatedly liken myself to a racehorse in the starting gate—bucking, snorting, and ready to run, but the gate was closed. To keep myself from becoming discouraged,

I had to remind myself that I needed to stay prepared because one day that gate *would* open. I believed that—like most events in the Kingdom—the breakthrough would come unexpectedly, suddenly; and I knew I had to be ready. When "due time" finally did arrive and we knew we were to start Catchfire! Ministries, I was prepared; and I haven't stopped running since!

Conclusion

Why have I spent so much time on Peter's restoration and the humility he developed? Because, as I stated before, humility is so glaringly absent in much of Christian leadership today. I know from experience that it is something we must put on every single day. May the examples of Barnabas and Peter inspire us. Surely these men will receive crowns of glory, but it would be impossible had they not clothed themselves with humility here on Earth. I am confident that every member of the *Glory Crown Crowd* in heaven will have excelled in humility. It is the mark of all true champions for Christ and an essential component of the *Barnabas Factor*. Remember, it does not matter how good we are at wielding the Sword of the Spirit if we are not also wearing the *cloak of humility*. Without it, we merely swing our swords in thin air, our efforts rendered powerless and ineffective.

Think now about the words of John the Baptist when Jesus the Christ approached him at the River Jordan. "He

The Cloak of Humility

[Jesus] must become greater; I must become less" (John 3:30). If you think about it, this was an amazing statement for him to make at that point in his life. John's ministry was at its peak and he had a huge following, yet he willingly laid it all down so that the spotlight would shift to where it belonged—on Jesus! John understood his place and his call, and he readily submitted to it. He put the cause of the Kingdom before his own ministry and reputation.

Be encouraged. Developing humility is something all believers must do. Everyone has been guilty of the vain sin of pride at one time or the other, but just as the Lord transformed Peter from proud to humble and took him from defeat to becoming a champion, He can do the same with you. But it does not come through osmosis. You must take the first step and seek humility. Then, as you clothe yourself with it every day, God will do the rest!

As we have traveled through this book together, I trust that you have grown in your awareness of how vital it is to establish your foundation on Christ and to be deeply rooted in Him. With those things solidly in place in your life, what's next? How about your destiny! We will focus on it in the final chapter.

> *Lord, I confess that I have allowed pride into my life, but I repent of it now. I know that without You, I am nothing. Help me to develop true humility, to wear it like a cloak every single day; and when pride comes near, help me to recognize it and cast it down. I pray that grace would be multiplied to me as I grow in humility, and I thank You in*

advance for the promotion You promise to grant me in due season. Amen.

CHAPTER 15

What's Next?

HAVE YOU EVER HEARD THE EXPRESSION, "All dressed up but nowhere to go"? This aptly describes where we are in our study on identity and security. Now that you have a thorough understanding of God's design and you are endeavoring to settle these issues in your life, it is now time to talk about your destiny!

We have established in this book that our most basic needs are to be accepted by God and to find our identity and security in Christ. This leads to the fourth most basic need of every person—to know our purpose in life. So, what is your purpose?

To find the answer, let me start by asking you a question: Why did God save you in the first place? Did He do it just so you could go to heaven and spend eternity with Him? If that were the only reason, He would have just taken you on to heaven when you first committed your life to Jesus. Why then did He leave you here on this planet?

My Story

I firmly believe there is an ultimate destiny and purpose for every person's life. I would like to share with you my story.

When I was eighteen years old, I began praying a rather dangerous prayer. "If You are pleased with me, teach me Your ways so I may know You and continue to find favor with You." I actually borrowed this prayer from Moses in Exodus 33:13. In addition I earnestly and faithfully prayed that the Lord would make His desires my desires, His thoughts my thoughts, and His passion my passion. You know what happened? God answered these prayers and the cry of my heart, but He did not do it in the way I expected.

After nearly ten years of daily praying these things, I found myself in the "bush" of Kenya, East Africa, bouncing along in the front seat of a four-wheel-drive pickup truck with a Canadian missionary and an aged Kenyan pastor. This pastor was in his seventies, but still rode his bicycle for miles at a time to check on churches in southwestern Kenya.

What's Next?

While the missionary continued wrestling with the deep ruts in the "road," the aged pastor asked me if I would come back to Kenya to help him pastor the pastors of the back country. My reply was fairly typical. I answered that I would if God called me to do it.

After a long pause, the elderly pastor then asked, "Hasn't God already called you to preach the Gospel?"

I answered that indeed He had!

After a second pause, the pastor continued, "If God has called you once, why do you need another call?"

I was speechless, to say the least. After a few moments of awkward silence on my part, both the missionary and the pastor laughed out loud. I did too, but that question had pierced my heart and I never forgot it. In fact, the more I thought about it, the more I realized that the wise Kenyan pastor was right. God had already called me. Besides that, He had already spelled out in Scripture that His desire is for us to reach the lost.

Around this same time in my life, the Holy Spirit had been highlighting scriptures like 2 Peter 3:9: "The Lord is not slow in keeping his promise, as some understand slowness. He is patient with you, not wanting anyone to perish, but everyone to come to repentance." As I continued to pray Exodus 33:13, God began teaching me that His passion is for no one to perish but for *all* come to know His love for them.

As we continued to bounce along on that dirt road in Kenya, I also reflected on my college years, where I had roomed with a guy preparing to become a missionary to the Muslim world. (Incidentally, he has been fulfilling that dream ever since we graduated.) His life greatly influenced my understanding of missions and God's passion for the lost.

My thoughts then drifted to the years after college when I worked for Pastor Bob Pate, whom I told you about earlier in the book. Having previously been a missionary to Brazil, he still possessed a love for the nations. He preached about them, prayed for them, and went regularly himself. In fact it was he who took me on my first mission trip. We went to Costa Rica in Central America.

As I contemplated these memories and thought about all I had learned since I first began praying Exodus 33:13, I prayed another dangerous prayer. In the front seat of that pickup, I uttered under my breath, "Father, I will go wherever You lead me and do whatever You desire me to do. I will even move to Kenya if that is Your will for my life."

Today, almost fifteen years later, I have traveled to more than forty nations, been overseas nearly one hundred times, and won people to the Lord on nearly every continent. My life has taken a turn that I never expected it to take, but it is totally awesome to think that I am part of the heartbeat of God to fulfill His vision and passion for planet Earth.

What's Next?

What Is Your Story?

You may be thinking right now, *Hal, that's great for you because you are called to go to the nations.* Yes, but like that wise Kenyan pastor stated, I only received one call and that is to preach. God spelled out the rest in His Word. You see, reaching the lost around the world is not a job for a select few. It is the *Great Commission* that Jesus gave the Church as a whole and to every believer specifically: "Go into all the world and preach the Good News to everyone, everywhere" (Mark 16:15 NLT 96).

Nowhere does it say that this is only a call for a select few missionaries or pastors. Just as salvation is not exclusive, neither is the spreading of the salvation message. It is for all believers! Look at what Jesus said.

> "You will receive power when the Holy Spirit comes on you; and you will be my witnesses in Jerusalem, and in all Judea and Samaria, and to the ends of the earth."
>
> Acts 1:8

Usually when we read this verse, the focus is on the fact that the Holy Spirit fills each believer with the power to be a witness. But *where* are we to be His witnesses? According to what Jesus said here, we are to be witnesses from where we are to the ends of the earth. Notice that this witness is to be simultaneous. All believers are to be witnesses in their

Jerusalem (hometown), Judea (home nation), Samaria (other nations), and to the ends of the earth—all at the same time!

But how can you do that since you are only one person who cannot be in two places at once? It's actually easier than you might think. You can do it through your prayers, your finances, going on short-term trips, and even by living full time overseas. Perhaps God is stirring your heart to become a missionary as you read this book. The bottom line is that there is a place for every believer in reaching the nations for Jesus, and each is equally important!

Knowing that, allow me to ask you this question again: Why did God leave you here and not take you to heaven after your salvation experience? To be His witness! He blessed you with salvation, and He in turn expects you to share that blessing with others—here and around the world! Take a few minutes to read Genesis 12:1–3, keeping in mind that you are the seed of Abraham, and let it inspire you.

What is your part in reaching the nations? Why not do as I did and begin to pray Exodus 33:13 daily and ask the Lord to reveal it to you. Ask Him when, where, and how you are to make your contribution to reach the lost in your own country and around the world? I promise that you will never receive true fulfillment in life until you take part in God's passion. It is the reason you are living now, on planet Earth. It might comfort you to know that Jesus even prayed about this in what is often referred to as His high priestly prayer: "My prayer is not that you take them out of the world but that you protect them from the evil one" (John 17:15). We are still here because He wants us to be His witnesses.

This is another area where Barnabas set an excellent example for us. After participating in the revival at Antioch, he did not just sit idle and concentrate on how blessed he was. He knew the heart of God was to spread the message to the nations, so he grabbed Paul and they set out on their first missionay journey, at the Holy Spirit's prompting, of course. I believe that is the natural flow for all believers who begin to understand their place and calling in the Kingdom of God. We come to a place where it is no longer about us and our needs, but it is all about reaching others and pleasing the Father. Our focus shifts outward. For many this will involve making significant changes in their lives. It may even involve a total paradigm shift in thinking. We cannot, however, make that shift properly unless the identity issue is settled, meaning the *Barnabas Factor* is firmly established in us.

The Two Seas

A powerful analogy can be drawn from the two seas within the borders of Israel—the Sea of Galilee and the Dead Sea. To the north is Galilee. It is arguably one of the most beautiful spots on Earth, especially at the traditional site of Jesus' Sermon on the Mount. The Sea of Galilee is actually a large, freshwater lake that abounds with fish and is a major commercial center in Israel. Life, in all its many forms, surrounds the Sea of Galilee. The Jordan River, which flows through the sea from north to south, is the chief water source, but it is also fed by underground springs.

If you travel along the Jordan River to the south, you will eventually run into the Dead Sea, which is at the lowest spot on Earth. Vastly different than the area surrounding the Sea of Galilee, the area around the Dead Sea is barren and rocky. The sea itself is just as its name describes—dead! Nothing much lives in it. Interestingly, the mineral content of this sea is so high that you actually float in it.

These two seas are fairly close in proximity and are fed by the same river, yet they are immensely different. One represents vibrant life and the other death and desolation. What is the difference? The Dead Sea unlike the Sea of Galilee has no outlet. The Jordan flows into it and stops there.

This is what happens to believers who never give out and stay inward in their focus. These believers have an "us four and no more" mentality and eventually become like the Dead Sea. Their souls become barren and desolate, yet they do not know why. One way you can tell if you are part of this group is to examine your prayer life. What is it that you spend the majority of your time praying about? For most believers, their prayers primarily consist of asking God to meet their own needs. While God earnestly desires for us to seek Him for our needs, He also wants us to pray for the needs of others.

What's Next?

On the other hand, there are those who realize it is not all about them; their focus is outward. These clearly see life from God's perspective and understand that they are an important part of His vision to reach the nations. I like to call these believers *Great Commission Christians.* These are fewer in number than the self-centered believers, but they are constantly praying for and reaching out to minister to others. As a resuilt, they are like the Sea of Galilee, full of life, vibrancy, and fruitfulness. Everywhere they go, they spread this abundant life. Barnabas was this kind of believer, providing a steady flow of encouragement to all with whom he came into contact. It is no wonder that every church he visited grew under his influence. You never hear Great Commission Christians make comments like, "We have so many needs here, why are we sending our money overseas and praying for people we don't even know?" Rather, they correctly understand that God is not an either/or God—He expects us to be a witness here and around the world at the same time.

The believers at Antioch were Great Commission Christians. In fact I believe that one of the chief reasons that church remained strong for so many years is that it became a sending church to the nations. It is a fact, missions-oriented families and churches prosper. Whenever revival breaks out, the end result should be that the message is taken to the nations. Anything less will cause the revival to implode on itself rather than to explode to the masses who need it most. God wants to offer the world the same things

He offers to the Church. The key is to make the transition from revival to harvest, but precious few do.

Now, I am not saying that you are called to go live in a grass hut in Africa and eat grub worms for dinner every evening. That is a calling for a select few, but there is a specific place for you in God's eternal plan to reach the nations with His love. Some are called to *go* and some are called to *send* but all are called to *pray*. What about you? Are you one of the Great Commission Christians or has your focus been turned inward. If you are the latter, now would be a great time to make a switch. I guarantee you that you will never regret it, and living with no regrets is the only way to enjoy abundant life!

The Plan

Legend has it that when Jesus first returned to heaven after His ascension, He encountered the angel Gabriel. Gabe first said, "Master, You suffered terribly for people down there!"

"I did," Jesus replied.

"And," continued Gabriel, "do they all know how much You love them and everything that You did for them?"

"Oh, no," Jesus answered. "Not yet. Right now, only a handful of people in Palestine know."

What's Next?

Perplexed, Gabriel continued by asking, "So what have You done to make sure that all the people know about Your love for them?"

"Well, I have asked Peter, James, John, and few others to tell people about Me. Those who are told will in turn tell others, and the Gospel will eventually be spread to farthest reaches of the globe. Ultimately, all of mankind will hear about Me and what I have done on their behalf."

The great archangel was skeptical about this simple plan because he knew that people are unreliable. "Yes," he said, "but what if Peter, James, and John grow weary? What if people who come after them forget? And what if, way down in the twenty-first century, people get too busy to bother telling others about You? Haven't You come up with a backup plan?"

"No, Gabriel, I haven't made any other plans," Jesus answered. "I'm counting on them!"

It is true—Jesus is counting on *you!* You and I are equally important in fulfilling heaven's plan for Earth. Can He count on you?

The Original Plan

This plan of God did not just originate with the Great Commission. In fact, it was God's vision from the beginning when He told Adam and Eve, "Be fruitful and increase in number; fill the earth and subdue it. Rule over the fish of the sea and the birds of the air and over every living creature that moves on the ground" (Gen. 1:28).

After Lisa and I were first married, my dad used to quote this verse to us with a big smile on his face. We knew he was really saying that he wanted grandchildren, and for years, I only saw God's command in that light. I have come to see, however, that God was commanding Adam and Eve to do more than just populate the earth. According to this verse, God did not intend for the first couple to keep what they had just inside the boundaries of the Garden of Eden, but He desired for them to fill the earth with the knowledge of the One, true God.

What did they possess in the Garden? A wonderful relationship with the Lord! Adam walked and talked with God. His every need and whim was more than adequately met through that relationship. God's intent was for Adam and Eve to plant, if you will, Gardens of Eden all over the world. Then men and women everywhere could worship God in their own culturally distinctive ways. This was God's plan from the beginning, and it has *not* changed!

Perhaps this is one of the reasons why Adam and Eve fell so easily in the Garden of Eden. They were not doing what they had been commanded to do, but rather they were enjoying the blessings of the Garden too much and were not eager to spread it. *Idleness* is indeed the devil's workshop!

What's Next?

The Tree of Life

Throughout this book, I have used the analogy of a tree to describe our lives, and I want to conclude by mentioning the last tree used in Scripture. In fact it is recorded in the final chapter of the entire Bible.

> The angel showed me the river of the water of life, as clear as crystal, flowing from the throne of God and of the Lamb down the middle of the great street of the city. On each side of the river stood the tree of life, bearing twelve crops of fruit, yielding its fruit every month. And the leaves of the tree are for the healing of the nations.
>
> Revelation 22:1–2

This tree is located beside the *River of Life.* This is where we should be planted as well. Also notice how often this tree bears fruit. Twelve times a year! How often do trees normally bear fruit? Only once each year. Clearly God's plan is for us to be planted by the River of Life so that we, too, may bear fruit on a continual basis.

Did you know that the soil in which a tree is planted determines the flavor of the fruit from that tree? Coffee, for example, from Costa Rica tastes different than coffee from Guatemala or Hawaii. Why? The soil is different. By the same token, if you are planted by the River of Life, you will begin to taste like God! This reminds me of Psalm 34:8—"Taste and see that the Lord is good"! We taste of Him through our daily relationship with Him. But what about those who do not know Him? They will taste of the Lord and His goodness through *you* and the fruit that you bear!

Finally, notice what the leaves of this tree are to be used for: "the healing of the nations." Does this not reveal that part of your destiny is to provide healing and life for the nations? I believe it does! Unless you are involved in reaching the nations in one way or another, you cannot say that you have fulfilled your destiny in this life. It is an integral part of what it means to be a follower of Jesus Christ.

Final Word

At the end of our days, when we believers are in heaven, it will be crystal clear that the greatest thing any of us could have done on Earth was to reach others for Jesus. Actually, it should be apparent to us now because it is very plainly spelled out in Scripture. I trust that you are seeing it more clearly than ever before.

Let us be counted among those who are committed to revealing the heart of God to the world. Let us strive to obey Him and please Him in everything that we do. And let us be among those who, when we reach the gates of heaven, hear, "Well done, My good and faithful servant!" (Matt. 25:21.) In the whole scheme of things, isn't that the only thing that really matters?

What's Next?

My prayer is that you will hear the Lord beckoning to you to let His heart become your heart. The key is to shift your focus from yourself to Jesus and the world He died for. As I have repeatedly stated throughout this book, the only way you can do that is by first settling the identity issue—who are you? As your identity continues to be firmly rooted in Jesus Christ, you will become more and more like Barnabas, Paul, Peter, and so many other fruitful believers. You will bear fruit continually and take healing to the nations.

I believe it is fitting that we close with the following words from the apostle Paul:

> I have been crucified with Christ and I no longer live, but Christ lives in me. The life I live in the body, I live by faith in the Son of God, who loved me and gave himself for me.
>
> Galatians 2:20

> For you died, and your life is now hidden with Christ in God.
>
> Colossians 3:3

Lord, it is clear to me that Your ultimate goal is for all to come to the saving knowledge of Jesus. I want to be an active participant in fulfilling Your plan. Show me what my part is and I will faithfully do it. I realize that in order for me to ever be truly effective, I must continually look to You as my Source for acceptance, identity, security, and purpose. I thank You that as I do, I am being transformed into the image of Christ so that I can bear abundant fruit for Your glory. Amen.

A NOTE FROM THE AUTHOR

Catchfire! Ministries

P.O. Box 701676

Tulsa, OK 74170

www.catchfire.org

ABOUT THE AUTHOR

Hal Boehm (pronounced *beam*) is the founder and president of Catchfire! Ministries—a missions mobilizing organization whose vision is to *Catch the Church on fire for the Nations and to Catch the Nations on fire for Jesus!*

Hal has ministered in more than 40 nations through various avenues—mass crusades, pastor/leadership conferences, and short-term mission trips. In recent years, he has held mass crusades in the nations of Dominican Republic and Haiti. Each crusade has had between 20,000–50,000 people in attendance nightly. Thousands have responded to the Gospel message and hundreds have reported instantaneous healings. Blind eyes, cancers, and deafness are among the miracles that have been recorded.

Hal and his wife, Lisa, have led over 40 short-term mission trips to nearly every continent. Hal has also been a pastor, associate pastor, and youth pastor, as well as the director of a missionary training program where he trained over 130 full-time missionaries. Annually he ministers in churches throughout the United States in addition to his overseas ministry.

Hal received his Master of Divinity from Oral Roberts University's Graduate School of Theology where he graduated with Highest Honors. He was also selected as the Seminarian of the Year by the faculty and staff of the seminary.

Presently, Hal resides in Tulsa, Oklahoma, along with his wife and daughter, Isabella.

ENDNOTES

[1] *Webster's New Collegiate Dictionary* (Springfield, Massachusetts: G. & C. Merriam Co., 1979) p. 696.

[2] Millard Erickson, *Christian Theology* (Grand Rapids, MI: Baker Book House, 1985) pp. 789–791.

[3] Etymology found at http://dictionary.reference.com/search?q=enthusiasm (accessed September, 2006).

[4] A reference to teaching by Gary Chapman on the five basic ways people express and receive love.

[5] James Strong, *Strong's Exhaustive Concordance* (Grand Rapids, MI: Baker Book House, 1981) #G3749.

[6] See Acts 13:13.

[7] See chapter 2, the section entitled, "Understand the Context."

[8] Eusebius. *The Life Application Commentary Series.* Vol. 3, *Ecclesiastical History* (Carol Stream, IL: The Livingstone Corporation, 2000) p. 39.

[9] See chapter 11, the section entitled, "Paul's Transformation."